$\mathcal{B}$

Cambridge Student Guide

Shakespeare

King Lear

Celeste Flower

Series Editor: Rex Gibson

CAMBRIDGE
UNIVERSITY PRESS

CAMBRIDGE UNIVERSITY PRESS
Cambridge, New York, Melbourne, Madrid, Cape Town, Singapore, São Paulo

Cambridge University Press
The Edinburgh Building, Cambridge CB2 2RU, UK

www.cambridge.org
Information on this title: www.cambridge.org/9780521008181

First published 2002
4th printing 2005

Printed in the United Kingdom at the University Press, Cambridge

A catalogue record for this publication is available from the British Library

ISBN-13 978-0-521-00818-1 paperback
ISBN-10 0-521-00818-2 paperback

Cover image: © Getty Images/PhotoDisc

Contents

Introduction

Lear, once all-powerful, gives away his kingdom to his daughters Goneril and Regan, yet still demands of them unquestioning love and absolute obedience. But both daughters abuse him cruelly. He falls from the condition of king to that of the most wretched beggar, and in the storm on the heath he experiences a vision of humanity at its lowest and most elemental: 'the thing itself. Unaccommodated man'.

Through his suffering he recognises that he has 'ta'en / Too little care' of the plight of the poor, and he learns the value of love and forgiveness, expressed through his youngest daughter Cordelia whom he had angrily banished at the start of the play. But in Shakespeare's bleak ending, although Lear is reunited with Cordelia, he sees her murdered. He dies, but whether in despair or hope that Cordelia lives, the audience is left to decide.

King Lear has been variously described as a folk tale similar to *Cinderella*, as resembling a Greek tragedy in its depiction of physical and emotional suffering, as a Christian drama in which Lear is finally redeemed. It has also been interpreted as a drama that comments critically on the hierarchy of the Jacobean state, on patriarchy, on King James' belief in his divine right to rule, and on the political anxieties that characterised the end of Queen Elizabeth's reign: fears of civil war and of the division of the kingdom.

King Lear poses an abiding question: why do people pay to see a play that depicts human suffering, in which the innocent die, and justice seems thwarted? Many critics answer that it is because *King Lear* is the supreme example of Shakespeare's tragic genius. But they are sharply divided about the nature and causes of the tragedy.

Some claim it is a play primarily about society; about power, property and inheritance. In such a reading, Lear, Poor Tom, and the Fool, as outcasts in their wretchedness on the heath, become symbols of the alienated and dispossessed of society. In contrast, other critics see the play as portraying a world in which the gods are malicious or simply indifferent to humanity's fate. Yet others claim it is essentially a personal tragedy, about Lear's journey to redemption. They argue that the play portrays how human dignity is reduced and assaulted, but also shows the process of restoration and the power of love.

Commentary

Act 1 Scene 1

King Lear's closest advisers, the Earls of Kent and Gloucester, discuss the king's plans for abdication in favour of his daughters and their husbands. It seems that Lear has always favoured one son-in-law over the other, until now, when he appears to be regarding them with equal affection. Gloucester laughingly excuses Edmund's illegitimacy and reminds Kent that he has another (legitimate) son. His description of Edmund's mother is coarse and bawdy, not designed to spare the young man's feelings. Kent, however, is polite towards Edmund, who returns a formal reply, remarking that he will 'study deserving'. The phrase seems to show respect and deference towards Kent, but beneath the surface it suggests a deeper clue to Edmund's character and intentions.

The frame has been set for the main action of the scene: 'the division of the kingdom' (see pages 67–8). Lear arrives with his retinue, often staged as a ceremonial procession. Lear sets the tone of the occasion, stage-managing the events. His speech is full of imperatives, indicating his natural authority and his expectation of being obeyed. He emphasises his own royalty by using the pronoun 'we' instead of 'I' as he states his intentions. His speech is formal and measured, delivered in blank verse, which contrasts with the informal opening conversations in prose. Lear's status suggests that he must take centre stage, but wherever a production chooses to place him, his very presence commands attention.

The king declares his 'darker purpose': an abdication ceremony is about to take place. He gives three reasons for relinquishing his throne: great age, a desire to ensure future peace in the land and a wish to make a good marriage alliance for his youngest daughter. To determine what each daughter will receive, he has devised a contest for them:

> Which of you shall we say doth love us most,
> That we our largest bounty may extend
> Where nature doth with merit challenge?   (*lines 46–8*)

The conventions of both seniority and fairy tale are observed; Goneril, as eldest daughter, must reply first. But even before she speaks, the audiences (both the watching courtiers and those in the theatre) are aware that this will not be a fair trial of the daughters' love for their father. Gloucester's earlier words revealed that the king had already weighed the worth of his sons-in-law and now Lear tells the court 'that we have divided / In three our kingdom' (lines 32–33). Soon, when Lear points to the map of his kingdom, it will be seen that the lines are already drawn, but that the prescribed thirds are not equal. The king fully intends to offer his youngest daughter 'A third more opulent' than those of her sisters.

Each sister's response to her father's challenge reveals much about her individual character. Goneril and Regan do not deliver impromptu answers, but carefully crafted and rehearsed public speeches. Both older sisters recognise their public and political duty to respond to this test of their worth. They know that love cannot be measured, but also understand the need to participate in the spectacle of state occasions. So they satisfy their father with flattering and insincere replies. Each is rewarded with her 'ample third', ceremoniously bestowed by Lear himself. Then Cordelia sets everything out of joint. Her father asks:

> What can you say to draw
> A third more opulent than your sisters?   *(lines 80–1)*

'Nothing', replies Cordelia. It creates an intensely dramatic moment. The flow of the language (shown in the abrupt departure from verse in lines 82–4) and the ceremony itself are both fractured, and many productions stage a long silence as Lear and the onstage audience struggle to understand what they have heard.

Despite opportunities to change her answer, Cordelia refuses to supply a speech that will equal the flattery of her sisters. Eventually she places her duty to her father on an equal footing with duty to her future husband. Lear, angered beyond endurance at not hearing what he wants, casts her off. Cordelia has always been her father's favourite (lines 117 and 208–10) and his plans for the last years of his life were to rely exclusively upon her 'kind nursery'. In whatever ways the other courtiers react to Lear's angry outburst, only Kent attempts to intervene on Cordelia's behalf.

Lear will not be gainsaid. He takes back control. His speech is full of imperatives as he expresses his towering rage: 'Come not . . . Hence . . . avoid . . . Call'. He shares Cordelia's allotted portion between her sisters. The court looks on as the emblematic coronet (perhaps intended for his youngest daughter) is handed over to Albany and Cornwall, to be parted between them. The divided coronet is a striking visual image, symbolising the dysfunction and chaos that will follow the dividing of the kingdom.

Again Kent tries to intervene. Though his tone towards the king is 'unmannerly', he offers Lear the same qualities as Cordelia has offered: love, honour and obedience. He is rewarded in the same way, banished from Lear's court. Before he is roughly dismissed, Kent urges Lear to 'See better'. This is not the first time that the motif of sight has appeared (Goneril spoke of a love 'Dearer than eyesight'), and it will recur throughout the play to emphasise the themes of appearance versus reality and of sight and blindness in both literal and metaphorical senses.

Kent vows to 'shape his old course' elsewhere, leaving as Gloucester escorts the King of France and the Duke of Burgundy into Lear's presence. Cordelia's suitors have not witnessed her fall from favour, so Lear's statement that he hates her bewilders them. Burgundy is unwilling to change the terms of the original bargain, but France, like Kent, argues for Cordelia's goodness France cannot understand what Cordelia can have done 'to dismantle / So many folds of favour' with her father. Metaphors of dismantling, disrobing and casting off clothing will become increasingly important in this play as Lear's fortunes change. Although France speaks in the formal style of courtly love poetry, his sincerity and regard for Cordelia is genuine. She brings no dowry, but to him she is 'unprized precious'. Lear however will not bestow even a parting blessing on them.

The public ceremonies over, the bluster and pomp of Lear's presence removed, Cordelia takes leave of her sisters. Their exchange reveals much about the relationship between the three women. Cordelia expresses distrust of her sisters and suspects that they will not treat their father kindly. In response, both sisters contemptuously dismiss her words.

The scene ends as it began, with an intimate conversation in prose. Goneril and Regan reveal that their private attitudes toward Lear are quite different from the public declarations of love they have made. At the start of the scene, Gloucester and Kent noted the changes in the king. Now his elder daughters warily consider the implications of his 'unconstant starts' for themselves, and resolve to act immediately:

GONERIL If our father carry authority with such disposition as he
    bears, this last surrender of his will but offend us.
REGAN We shall further think of it.
GONERIL We must do something, and i'th'heat.   (lines 294–8)

Act 1 Scene 2

Edmund takes the stage alone. His soliloquy reveals his character, his grudge and his plan for advancement. He calls on Nature as his goddess. The laws of nature, not those of civilisation or society, are those he intends to live by, because society disinherits bastard children. Shakespeare's audience would recognise in Edmund's complaint references to their own prejudices wherein bastards were often rejected or ignored by their fathers and brought shame upon their mothers.

Edmund despises the way in which illegitimacy becomes equated with worthlessness and vile behaviour. He holds it as unreasonable that half-brothers should not share their father's wealth, particularly when the 'father's love is to the bastard . . . / As to th'legitimate'. Edmund has studied carefully the lesson in deserving taught by the 'love trial' in Scene 1. He has learnt that those who speak plainly, offering truth and sincere love, gain nothing. He has seen how inheritances can be abruptly granted or denied, and he plans to seize his brother's share of Gloucester's property:

Well then,
Legitimate Edgar, I must have your land.   (lines 15–16)

The similarity between the two families' situations has not evaded Edmund: as Goneril and Regan have profited, he too intends to possess his sibling's share by deception. Edmund has prepared a letter, supposedly written by his brother, which he will use to set his plans in train. He begins to read it as he hears his father approach. Gloucester appears perturbed by the oddity and topsy-turvy injustice of earlier events, but he will shortly commit a parallel injustice against his legitimate son. With deliberate irony, Edmund responds to his father's question 'What paper were you reading?' using Cordelia's exact words: 'Nothing, my lord'. Pretending to withhold the fake letter from his father with the purpose of protecting his brother, he reinforces his own virtue. When Gloucester insists on reading the letter he discovers (mistakenly) that Edgar plans to kill him. The gulling of Gloucester is complete when he concludes that his worst fears and superstitions are come about, and that Edgar is a murderous villain.

There are more parallels between this and the preceding scene. Gloucester's readiness to believe ill of his beloved child and refusal to listen to a reasonable defence mirrors Lear's outburst and dismissal of Cordelia. Yet Gloucester did not witness that angry episode, nor did he hear Kent's unsuccessful pleading on Cordelia's behalf; he cannot therefore hear the echo of Kent's words, 'My life I never held but as a pawn', in Edmund's feigned defence of his brother:

> I dare pawn down my life for him   *(lines 77–8)*

Edmund calculates every word he speaks to his father in order to show himself in a good light and throw doubt upon his innocent brother's honour. Gloucester leaves, gloomily seeing chaos everywhere, and entrusting Edmund to act against Edgar. Edmund, once again alone on stage, scorns Gloucester's superstitious misgivings, mocking any notion that the stars influence human nature. As Edgar arrives, he prepares to resume his acting role:

> Pat: he comes, like the catastrophe of the old comedy. My cue
> is villainous melancholy   *(lines 117–18)*

The theatrical terms he uses emphasise how staged his performance will be: the 'catastrophe' was the final event of a play or comedy; and Edmund takes his 'cue' and gesture from the old plays, too – 'with a sigh like Tom o'Bedlam' he begins to draw his brother into the trap.

The episode is usually played at speed, and Shakespeare's choice of prose here makes it easy for actors to deliver the lines rapidly. Edgar says little and is stage-managed by his brother throughout. Edmund advises his brother of their father's anger and suggests that he stay away from Gloucester. He will clear his brother's name, but until then Edgar must hide, or only go out armed with his sword. Edgar is shocked. He cannot think how he has offended his father and concludes that someone has deliberately lied about him. Nevertheless, he will follow his brother's advice, for like Gloucester he believes that Edmund is acting in his best interests.

Edmund's final comment shows contempt for his credulous father and his good-natured and unsuspecting brother. He is pleased: his plot is working out and he will do whatever it takes to achieve his ambitions. Edmund is not only the bastard by birth but is acting the Jacobean stereotype of the bastard by nature:

> Let me, if not by birth, have lands by wit.
> All with me's meet that I can fashion fit.   *(lines 155–6)*

Act 1 Scene 3

The action shifts to the home of Goneril and her husband, Albany. In Scene 1, Lear gave away his lands, dividing them between his two elder daughters. He must now rely on their hospitality and has arranged to spend alternate months with each one. He is an expensive house guest, for he keeps with him a following of a hundred knights. Goneril has endured the upheaval and costs for some time, but is now finding the unruly behaviour of her father's retinue too much to bear. Shakespeare makes her irritation clear in the first line:

> Did my father strike my gentleman for chiding of his fool?
> *(lines 1–2)*

This is the first mention of Lear's Fool. His master holds him in high regard, and the old king has physically assaulted his daughter's chief steward, Oswald, because he had rebuked the Fool. This is the excuse Goneril needs to evict her father and his troublesome adherents from her home. When she hears that Lear himself has struck her trusted servant, she decides to force the issue. Rather than reason with her father, she intends to snub him ('Say I am sick') and orders Oswald not to attend to Lear as carefully as before.

When the two sisters last spoke together, at the end of Scene 1, they were about to consider what to do in a situation such as this. It is now clear that they have agreed not to tolerate Lear's presence and conduct in their homes. Goneril now wants everything swiftly brought to a crisis. She commands Oswald and his fellow servants to stir up resentment:

And let his knights have colder looks among you:
What grows of it no matter. Advise your fellows so.

(lines 19–20)

She hopes that the action will bring on a clash between her household and Lear's followers. She will then be able to claim justification for what she plans to do. Meanwhile she will write a letter to advise Regan that she should act in a similar fashion when Lear and his followers arrive.

Act 1 Scene 4

Despite banishment, Kent remains loyal to Lear. To rejoin the old king's company, he has followed him to Goneril's home, but in disguise. This links to a major theme of the play: Kent, and other characters, cast off clothing (and with it their identity) to adopt different roles. In spite of being disguised, Kent will continue to speak plainly and will remain true to his nature and purpose to serve the king.

Lear returns from hunting and imperiously demands dinner. Although a guest in his daughter's house, he behaves as if he is the master of the house. When Kent presents himself to the old king as a stranger in need of employment he is invited to join the company. The question of authority, an attribute which Kent claims he sees in Lear's countenance, will be further addressed as the scene progresses. The first indication of the struggle for authority between Lear and Goneril is seen in the attentions of her household servants. Service is not swift enough for Lear. He again impatiently calls for dinner and demands to know where Goneril is. Oswald follows his mistress' instructions, deliberately ignoring Lear's question. A Knight, sent to follow Oswald, brings back the steward's surly message, and comments on how attitudes to Lear have changed in Goneril's household. His words prompt Lear himself to comment that he has noticed 'a most faint neglect of late'.

Lear's Fool will not answer his calls either. He is pining for Cordelia, a matter Lear does not wish to discuss. A confrontation takes place between the king and Oswald. Lear verbally abuses the steward, charges him with insolence and strikes him. Kent trips Oswald, then throws him out. The roughness of Kent's manner and actions, although fitting his newly adopted guise, will breed further resentment in Lear's daughters.

The Fool finally arrives as Lear rewards Kent for his assistance. He is swift to point out to Kent that he is a fool himself to follow Lear, rather than to attach himself to those now in power. The Fool's speech is of a riddling quality, loaded with inversions and images that reflect aspects of the story:

> this fellow has banished two on's daughters and did the third
> a blessing against his will   *(lines 88–90)*

Lear has, of course, banished only Cordelia, without even a blessing, and rewarded the other two daughters. But it is not a mistake of understanding on the Fool's part. Lear's third daughter, Cordelia, is now queen of France, blessed with a loving husband. Meanwhile, Goneril and Regan are planning to break down their father's power and authority. The Fool's version of the consequences of the 'love trial' mirrors Kent's view of the situation, expressed in Scene 1 (line 175), that 'Freedom lives hence, and banishment is here'.

In the exchanges that follow, the Fool's jokes and sayings comment caustically on Lear's decisions and behaviour. Fools were often employed in the palaces of royalty to provide amusement, and to make critical comment without fear of punishment (see page 121). In simple doggerel verse, the Fool offers painful personal advice in the style of old proverbs and wise sayings, and his first song carries a harsh lesson for Lear about the folly of giving away all one's lands. In spite of Lear's obvious affection for his Fool, the jokes come dangerously close to offending him. With a direct reminder of Cordelia's answer in Scene 1 (echoed also by Edmund in Scene 2), the Fool drives his point home. Yet Lear still cannot understand what he is being told and his reply to the Fool's question recalls that crucial earlier exchange with Cordelia:

FOOL Can you make no use of nothing, nuncle?
LEAR Why, no, boy; nothing can be made out of nothing.
FOOL [*To Kent*] Prithee, tell him so much the rent of his land comes
    to; he will not believe a fool.   *(lines 115–18)*

In a passage found only in the Quarto text (see pages 61–2) the Fool recites a rhyme about a sweet and a bitter fool. The rhyme is a clear and direct criticism of Lear's decision to give away his land. It immediately provokes an angry question and a derisive response:

LEAR Dost thou call me fool, boy?

FOOL All thy other titles thou hast given away; that thou wast born
with.   (Quarto, *following line 119*)

Other echoes of the opening scene resound in the Fool's talk of an egg
having two crowns. Not only do his words continue the money motif
begun in his first song but they bring to mind the coronet, symbol of
land and authority, given to be divided between the son-in-law dukes.
What follows further presses home the Fool's view that Lear has set
the natural order of things in reverse. The Fool complains that no
matter what he does he will be dealt with badly: his one consolation is
that he is only a half-wit and not completely brainless like his master:

I had rather be any kind o'thing than a fool, and yet I would
not be thee, nuncle; thou hast pared thy wit o'both sides and
left nothing i'th'middle.   (*lines 145–8*)

The Fool is spared censure by the arrival of Goneril with a face like
thunder, and he cannot resist further jabs at Lear, who has given
everything away to her, including his common sense. Goneril
launches into an aggrieved complaint against the Fool, the riotous
behaviour of Lear's knights and Lear's own approval of such insolent
behaviour. Her first four impatient lines suggest that she is about to
pick a quarrel with her father, but rather than launch into invective
she restrains her language at the very point when she is accusing her
father of lack of restraint in his behaviour and that of his followers.
She intends to restrict their activities, arguing that she must do so for
the good of everyone, not just herself. The Fool continues his
commentary alongside the exchange between father and daughter,
emphasising for the audience and for Lear a sense of impending
trouble.

Taken aback by Goneril's rebuke, Lear shows his disbelief by play-
acting that he is dreaming (in the same way that someone today might
say 'pinch me, I must be dreaming'). Goneril rejects this as another of
her father's childish games ('new pranks'), urging him to act his age
and make an effort to understand her intentions. She again complains
of the behaviour of his debauched followers, and demands that he
should dismiss 'A little' of his train and surround himself with just a
few respectable retainers. Lear explodes:

> Darkness and devils!
> Saddle my horses; call my train together. –
> Degenerate bastard, I'll not trouble thee;
> Yet have I left a daughter.   *(lines 207–10)*

Goneril continues to complain about Lear and his followers' violent and unacceptable behaviour. Albany enters, amazed by the incident and unaware of its making. Lear turns his invective upon his daughter again:

> Thou marble-hearted fiend,
> More hideous when thou show'st thee in a child
> Than the sea-monster.   *(lines 214–16)*

He accuses her of ingratitude, the same 'small fault' as Cordelia had shown towards him. With the memory of his best-loved daughter, he begins to realise that he has made terrible errors of judgement. Lear invokes Nature to curse Goneril with sterility or monstrous children, then rushes out. He returns almost at once, distressed that half his men have been dismissed. He curses Goneril again, fighting back the tears he does not want to shed. His words once again express the recurring theme of physical and moral blindness:

> Old fond eyes,
> Beweep this cause again, I'll pluck ye out
> And cast you with the waters that you loose
> To temper clay.   *(lines 256–9)*

Lear departs in extreme anger, intending to call upon the hospitality of Regan, who he believes will comfort and restore him. The dramatic irony is that Regan and Goneril are single-minded in their malign plans for their father.

Once Lear has left, Albany remonstrates with his wife for her behaviour towards her father, but she cuts him short, calls for her steward and sends the Fool packing. She argues that her father was running a private army and, given his quarrelsome nature and the onset of senility, she fears that he might 'hold our lives in mercy'. Goneril has already prepared a message to Regan and sends it post-haste with her most trusted servant.

The brief exchange between husband and wife reveals their distinctive characters, and also highlights an important aspect of the play: trust versus fear.

ALBANY Well, you may fear too far.
GONERIL   Safer than trust too far.

(line 282)

Their final exchange throws further light on their contrasting characters. Just as Lady Macbeth suspects that her husband is 'too full o' the milk of human kindness' to be ruthless in his ambition (*Macbeth* Act 1 Scene 5, line 15), so Goneril accuses Albany of being too forgiving and unwise in his 'milky gentleness':

> No, no, my lord,
> This milky gentleness and course of yours,
> Though I condemn not, yet under pardon
> You are much more ataxed for want of wisdom,
> Than praised for harmful mildness.   *(lines 294–8)*

Goneril will not give up her plan to assume power over her father even though Albany doubts whether her fears about the future are justified. He cautions that well-intended actions can result in making things worse. But Goneril is unmoved, and Albany, seeing it is futile to argue, decides to await how things turn out:

ALBANY How far your eyes may pierce I cannot tell;
                Striving to better, oft we mar what's well
GONERIL Nay then –
ALBANY Well, well, th'event.   *(lines 299–302)*

Act 1 Scene 5

As he sets out for Regan's home, Lear sends a letter in advance to announce his coming. Kent is to carry it, but is warned to say nothing of what has passed at Goneril's house. The Fool's jokes make Lear laugh, but they also contain a warning: Lear may be trusting too much to Regan's kindness for she is 'as like this [her sister] as a crab's like an apple' (a crab apple resembles other apple fruits very closely). Through the Fool's puns and jokes, Lear increasingly realises his mistakes. When Lear says 'I did her wrong' (line 20), he is thinking not of Goneril, but of Cordelia. There has been no direct prompt to make him think of her but, as shown in the previous scene, Lear has her much in mind:

> O Lear, Lear, Lear!
> Beat at this gate that let thy folly in
> And thy dear judgement out.   *(Scene 4, lines 225–7)*

Although he answers the Fool's riddles there is a sense in which Lear is not really listening to him, but is instead obsessed with recent events:

> So kind a father!   *(line 27)*

> To take't again perforce. Monster ingratitude!   *(line 32)*

Startled from his thoughts by the Fool's suggestion that he should be beaten for lack of wisdom, Lear voices his deepest fear:

> O let me not be mad, not mad, sweet heaven!   *(line 37)*

With Lear's retinue ready to depart, the Fool speaks a final couplet. Behind its apparent sexual meaning is a message to the audience: if they have ignored the deeper meanings of his jokes until now then they will not be able to remain naive when they experience the events that follow:

> She that's a maid now, and laughs at my departure,
> Shall not be a maid long, unless things be cut shorter.
>   *(lines 42–3)*

Act 1: Critical review

Act I establishes two parallel plots. The first is set in motion by Lear's desire to relinquish his throne in favour of his daughters, dividing his wealth and kingdom between them. The second concerns the Gloucester family and is the story of a brother who sets out to fool his father and rob his sibling of his inheritance.

The ceremonial atmosphere of Scene 1 thinly hides the absurdity of the 'love trial' set up by Lear for his daughters. The ritual is fractured by Cordelia's refusal to conform to her father's will. Even when urged to 'See better', Lear cannot separate pretence from reality, a rehearsed speech from a spontaneous reply. Unable to distinguish truth from flattery, he rejects both his loyal daughter and loyal courtier, Kent. Lear's blindness to the truth initiates important themes of the play, appearance versus reality, and both physical and moral blindness, that will be expressed in recurring motifs and metaphors throughout the play.

Scene 2 introduces the Gloucester plot, echoing themes already established: sibling rivalry and the relationship between parent and child. The similarities between Lear and Gloucester are evident. Both mistake what they hear for the truth, and are swift to believe ill of a beloved child, blind to the reality before them. Just as Lear banishes Cordelia, so Gloucester mistakes the true nature of his honest son Edgar and favours the wicked, deceiving Edmund.

The remaining scenes return to the Lear plot. Lear is angered by his eldest daughter's challenge to his authority, and in his violent reaction to Goneril's remonstrance he begins to recognise his mistake. Throughout, the Fool comments sardonically on all he sees and hears. He persistently emphasises that Lear's own folly is responsible for his distress.

Expecting succour from his second daughter, Lear sets out to lodge with Regan, and the Fool points out to him what is already obvious to the audience: Regan has professed herself to be 'of that self-mettle' as her sister.

Act I establishes the characters and their good or bad natures. The dissemblers have deceived the king and the earl, whose tragic journeys have begun in earnest.

Act 2 Scene 1

The events of Act 2 take place at Gloucester's castle, towards which many characters are travelling. Edmund learns of the imminent arrival of Regan and the Duke of Cornwall. Rumour has it that Cornwall and Albany may yet be planning 'likely wars' between each other, the kind of 'future strife' Lear wished to prevent by dividing his kingdom in the play's opening scene. Secretly Edmund is pleased to hear the news.

As in their previous encounter, conversation between the brothers is one-sided. Edgar has little chance to question what his seemingly honest brother tells him. He is dumbfounded by the suggestion that he has slandered the two dukes, and follows Edmund's directions to ensure his personal safety. His confusion is compounded by the relative darkness of their meeting place and by Edmund's urgent whispering, which suddenly gives way to shouting and confrontation. He flees, and Edmund wounds himself to make Edgar seem even more of a villain.

Edmund's cries bring Gloucester and servants carrying torches. The father seems more interested in apprehending the fugitive son than in tending to the one who bleeds. What Edmund says of his brother is a reminder of his own opening words at the beginning of Act 1 Scene 2, where he called upon Nature:

> Here stood he in the dark, his sharp sword out,
> Mumbling of wicked charms, conjuring the moon
> To stand auspicious mistress.   *(lines 37–9)*

Edmund alleges that his brother tried to incite him to murder Gloucester, forcing him to defend himself and scare Edgar away. Gloucester calls none of Edmund's account into question, so in full knowledge of the irony his words carry, Edmund reports how his brother taunted that no one would believe his story. Edmund takes great care to set up a foil for every denial that his brother might make, even down to denying the handwriting ('character') of the letter he shows to Gloucester, in order to make his own case appear even more convincing. Gloucester is completely taken in and orders Edgar's exile or death:

> Not in this land shall he remain uncaught;
> And found, dispatch   *(lines 56–7)*

Edgar's position can be likened to Kent's banishment, which Gloucester himself considered had been ordered 'Upon the gad'. When he vows to set up a reward for Edgar to be captured and executed, Gloucester does not realise how closely he imitates Lear's haste and error. Like his bastard son, he too sees the Duke of Cornwall's arrival as an opportunity to achieve an end, in this case gaining the authority to post 'Wanted' notices. He intends to reward Edmund's loyalty by acknowledging him as his legal heir:

> Loyal and natural boy, I'll work the means
> To make thee capable *(lines 83–4)*

Regan and Cornwall arrive, on the pretext of seeking Gloucester's advice. Regan has heard of the rift between her father and sister, and she intends to meet Goneril here. Meanwhile, when Lear arrives at Cornwall's palace, he will find no one at home.

Cornwall already knows of Edgar's flight from the castle and, praising Edmund's apparent sense of duty to his father, takes him into his service. The audience will be fully aware of the irony in Cornwall's assessment of Edmund's character: 'Natures of such deep trust we shall much need' (line 115). But his observation is also a further hint that there may be unrest between the two dukes. Cornwall is gathering his allies, relying on Gloucester's support because the earl is independently wealthy and his castle is a valuable stronghold. In any case, Gloucester has already acknowledged Cornwall as his 'master' and 'patron' (lines 57–8).

It is vital to note the twisted manner in which information is relayed. The most recent event is the suspected treachery and disappearance of Edgar, which Regan swiftly comments upon. She perceives it not as an isolated event, but as something intrinsically linked to her own preoccupations. She skilfully implicates her father by stressing his relationship to Edgar.

> What, did my father's godson seek your life?
> He whom my father named, your Edgar? *(lines 90–1)*

She also links Edgar with the 'riotous knights' whose actions have so inflamed her sister. There has been no suggestion until now that Edgar is a member of Lear's retinue, but Edmund, who always has an eye for a chance to further blacken his brother's name, is swift to confirm that he was. Regan's warped interpretation of events and her view of the corruption of Lear's knights have been entirely coloured by the report of events in her sister's letter.

Act 2 Scene 2

Kent and Oswald, both acting as messengers, meet in the courtyard of Gloucester's castle. Kent instantly recognises Goneril's steward and begins to rail at him for carrying letters full of dishonest reports of King Lear. He deliberately picks a quarrel, then insults him in a torrent of abusive descriptions, claiming to see him for what he is; a lowborn servant, self-seeking and mercenary (see page 68).

The dispute expresses a major motif of the play: that things are not as they seem. In his disguise, Kent might look like a servant, but unlike Oswald, Kent is a nobleman, highborn and independently wealthy. Being noble by nature, he remains loyal to his master the king. Kent has deliberately abased himself to remain by Lear's side, and thus his character contrasts with the self-seeking natures of Edmund and Oswald.

Kent's anger springs from his strong sense that Goneril, personified as 'Vanity the puppet', shows no respect to her father in the letters she sends. He attacks Oswald, and the noise brings household and guests running, Edmund arriving first. Stepping in to part them, he too is invited to fight. Cornwall tries to discover the cause of the disagreement, but Kent does not state a clear case against Oswald. Instead, he claims a simple hatred of opposites. His answers to Cornwall are frank and impertinent:

> I have seen better faces in my time
> Than stands on any shoulder that I see
> Before me at this instant.   *(lines 83–5)*

Cornwall seems to ignore the barb of Kent's contemptuous remark, describing him as being the kind of man who exploits a reputation for frank speaking in order to conceal dishonest, devious intentions. Cornwall considers a man like this to be more crafty than obsequious servants who, when they bow, seem to imitate the actions of ducks, bobbing their heads and stretching their necks in turn. Kent denies being the crafty type Cornwall has described. He adapts his speech, taking on an altogether different 'garb' to mock at the style of flatterers:

> Sir, in good faith, in sincere verity,
> Under th'allowance of your great aspect,
> Whose influence like the wreath of radiant fire
> On flick'ring Phoebus' front   *(lines 95–8)*

Flattery is easy: just claim to speak truth in redundant phrases, use superlatives, make comparisons with great Classical figures such as the sun-god Phoebus, crowned with flame! Cornwall is bewildered by Kent's speech. When Kent speaks again, Shakespeare gives him prose to mark another change in speaking style. Kent regrets that Cornwall dislikes his manner, but he denies flattery in plain terms: 'I know, sir, I am no flatterer.'

Cornwall turns to Oswald to discover what he did to provoke attack. Oswald protests his innocence and refers to the time when he was tripped. He claims that Kent received praise from the king for that action and was so pleased with himself that he could not resist another attempt. Kent murmurs his opinion:

> None of these rogues and cowards
> But Ajax is their fool.   *(lines 113–14)*

His meaning seems obscure. The remark could be aimed at Oswald, who will make a fool of Cornwall if the duke takes Oswald's word. It might be an insult pitched at Cornwall, comparing him with the foolish Greek warrior, Ajax, or even with a lavatory ('a jakes' in Jacobean slang). It is not clear either quite what prompts Cornwall's anger, but by now he is tired of trying to establish what has caused the brawl, and he has only to pick out the words 'rogues', 'cowards' and 'fool' from Kent's muttering to be further incensed.

Cornwall takes Oswald's part and calls for the stocks. Kent protests that this punishment of the king's messenger shows a lack of reverence towards the king himself. Gloucester also fears Lear's reaction to Cornwall's judgement. But Regan, who has already taken delight in extending the period of Kent's punishment, makes it clear that the two dukes and their wives now wield authority, not the old king.

Alone on stage in the stocks, Kent's final words are both proverbial and prophetic. He realises that events are taking a bad turn, as much for Lear as for himself. The rising sun provides light for him to read a letter that he carries. It is from Cordelia, who knows that he is disguised and with her father's retinue. The letter promises that she will restore her father's 'Losses' if she can. Before sinking into exhausted sleep, Kent asks Fortune, the goddess of luck, to turn her wheel. If the fortunes of the king are near the bottom of the wheel, continued turning will eventually bring him to better times.

Act 2 Scene 3

The dramatic effectiveness of Edgar's soliloquy is increased if the audience witnesses his actual transformation from the son of an earl to a beggar. In some productions Edgar casts off his sumptuous court clothing, replacing it with the blanket-stuff of a beggar. In others, he appears already disguised, sometimes begrimed and almost naked. The disguise he adopts is that of the Bedlam beggars of Shakespeare's time, released from hospital with permission to seek alms. Their naked arms and legs were often scarred, where they had torn at their own flesh. Edgar tries out his new 'accents' and steps into exile with a new identity:

> 'Poor Turlygod! Poor Tom!'
> That's something yet: Edgar I nothing am.　　　　*(lines 20–1)*

Throughout this scene, Kent is still on stage, asleep in the stocks. His presence serves as a visual reminder that loyalty to Lear has led him to abase himself, disguising his appearance, his accent and his manner. It has also led to his punishment in the stocks. As such Kent stands as a pattern for Edgar: both use disguise for self-preservation, both risk death if they are caught and discovered, and Edgar, like Kent, now embarks upon an act of self-abasement through disguise of appearance, accent and manner. As the play progresses, Kent's loyalty will be paralleled in the great loyalty Edgar will show to his father, Gloucester.

Act 2 Scene 4

Lear's arrival wakes the sleeping Kent. Though the Fool jokes about Kent's wooden stockings ('nether-stocks'), Lear is not amused by what he sees. As predicted, he is affronted by the disrespect shown, considering it 'worse than murder'. Kent's straightforward explanation to his master contrasts starkly with the mocking answers he gave to Cornwall in Scene 2.

The Fool's proverbial statement and rhyme emphasise that things are getting worse for Lear. What seems like a simple proverb based on migration patterns of wild geese may be Shakespeare's reference to a contemporary lawsuit in which a nobleman's daughter, Lady Wildgoose, tried to take over the running of her father's assets (see pages 64–5). The message of the Fool's rhyme is that a child's love for its father is conditional on his wealth, and that impoverished fathers have ungrateful and unfeeling children.

Lear is so moved by what he hears and sees that he almost succumbs to a fit of weeping: '*Hysterica passio!*' He attempts to regain control of his emotions by action and by commanding others: 'Follow me not, stay here.' Lear has arrived at Gloucester's palace with a much reduced retinue, and Kent notices the diminished number. The Fool uses winter as a symbol of ill fortune and hard times to explain that as Lear's men have realised that his power is dwindling, they have left to follow their own self-interests. But the Fool stresses that he will remain loyal to his master:

> But I will tarry, the fool will stay,
> And let the wise man fly;
> The knave turns fool that runs away,
> The fool no knave, perdy.   *(lines 75–8)*

When Lear returns to the stage with Gloucester, his anger and resentment are made clear through the repetitions in his speech of 'they' (lines 81–2). He has lost patience with his son-in-law and daughter, which shows as he indignantly picks up on the words 'fiery' and 'quality' in Gloucester's description of Cornwall. Repeated phrases indicate that he is impatient with Gloucester too: '"Informed them"?', 'I'd speak with . . .', 'The king would speak with . . .', 'the dear father / Would with his daughter speak'.

He insists upon obedience to his wishes, and peppers his language with imperatives: 'Fetch', 'Commands', 'Tell', 'Give me', 'Go tell', 'bid', 'come forth', 'hear me'. In the midst of his rising fury, Lear does attempt to make allowance for his son-in-law, suddenly wondering whether he is being kept waiting because Cornwall is ill: 'maybe he is not well'. But the sight of Kent still in the stocks persuades Lear that he is being deliberately refused and defied. His hysteria resurfaces:

> Death on my state! Wherefore
> Should he sit here? *(lines 105–6)*

Lear's brief attempt to be considerate ('I'll forbear') signally fails. As Gloucester leaves to find the duke and duchess, the Fool jokes about two cockneys whose acts of consideration and kindness were quite misguided.

The entrance of Cornwall and Regan can have great dramatic impact. It is discussed in detail on pages 107–13. Lear's emotional state is reflected in the breathless fractured rhythms of his speech as he labours to explain to Regan what has happened. She defends her sister's interests, suggesting that her father is now too old to judge what is best for him and should return to Goneril. Lear is incredulous and mockingly sinks to his knees as if to plead with his eldest daughter. He flatters Regan, saying she is quite unlike her sister. The sight of Kent or the empty stocks reminds Lear that he still has not discovered who it was that insulted him, but his question 'Who put my man i'th'stocks?' is ignored as Regan and Cornwall turn their attention to Goneril's arrival. Lear will ask his question twice more before he receives an answer to it.

The actor-critic Harley Granville Barker suggested that this moment in the play, as Regan greets Goneril, represents the nadir (lowest point) of Lear's fortunes. As he suggests, this point can be emphasised by clear blocking (how actors are positioned on stage in relation to one another) to suggest personal and political commitments and loyalties:

> On the one side stand Goneril and Regan and Cornwall in all authority. The perplexed Gloucester stands a little apart. On the other side is Lear, the Fool at his feet, and his one servant, disarmed, freed but a minute since, behind him.

There are many other possibilities, and movements can add important nuances. Goneril might deliberately ignore her father, moving straight to her sister. She might bow to or acknowledge Cornwall first, rather than Lear. Gloucester could tentatively move towards the king. The Fool need not be at Lear's feet at all. If Kent is still on stage, he might be at Lear's elbow now, perhaps providing physical support to his master.

Wherever they stand on stage, the sisters and Cornwall are shoulder to shoulder in spirit and purpose. They assume authority and set out the terms of Lear's continued stay with them. Knowing their collective strength, they quickly make it clear that they are no longer content with simply reducing his train, but wish him to dismiss it altogether. They know their father well enough to anticipate his reaction: he will 'abjure all roofs' rather than surrender to their terms.

Lear now struggles to make sense of the blows dealt by his daughters to his security and dignity. He fights for self-control, seeking the best deal for himself and his retinue, but only compounds the mistakes he made in the play's opening scene as he again tries to assess love in measurable terms, telling Goneril 'thou art twice her love'. The daughters' hard-heartedness is starkly revealed in their callous questioning of Lear's need for companions of his own choosing:

GONERIL   Hear me, my lord:
    What need you five and twenty? ten? or five?
    To follow in a house where twice so many
    Have a command to tend you?
REGAN   What need one?   *(lines 253–6)*

Regan's three cruel words strike home. Lear passionately rejects the notion that human need can be determined by precise calculation: 'O reason not the need!' He asserts that if our requirements are no more than the very basic necessities, then human life is worth no more than an animal's. Regan's fine clothes are superfluous to her natural needs:

    Allow not nature more than nature needs,
    Man's life is cheap as beast's. Thou art a lady;
    If only to go warm were gorgeous,
    Why nature needs not what thou gorgeous wear'st,
    Which scarcely keeps thee warm.   *(lines 259–63)*

In these exchanges with Goneril and Regan, Lear comes to the shocking realisation that his daughters are of like mind. Yet he refuses to be brought to tears by them. As his anger and emotional turmoil increase, a storm breaks, dramatically reflecting the passion Lear experiences. Rain pours down just as Lear himself cannot weep. He vows revenge on the two 'unnatural hags', and leaves with his few followers, fearing for his sanity:

> O fool, I shall go mad. *(line 279)*

The sisters are resolved not to take in any of Lear's followers, and Goneril tells Gloucester to offer no further hospitality to Lear. Regan, more unkind still, displays her lack of compassion for her father. He must learn the hard way, from his mistakes:

> O sir, to wilful men,
> The injuries that they themselves procure
> Must be their schoolmasters. *(lines 295–7)*

To ensure that the lesson Lear teaches himself is harsh in the extreme, Regan orders 'Shut up your doors'. Cornwall approves the finality of his wife's command. Those left behind in the castle courtyard must also take shelter from the night and the approaching storm. His words of advice to Gloucester, 'come out o'th'storm', are ominous given events to come in Act 3.

Act 2: Critical review

In this act, characters emerge with even more striking clarity and take up their position in one of two camps: there seems to be a clear division between those who are good and those who are evil. By the end of the act, those in the latter camp have assumed the power and authority they seek.

As the main players converge on Gloucester's house, so certain major themes and issues of the play are developed. Family relationships take new turns, with sister allied to sister against father, replacing the support they had feigned towards his authority at the start of Act 1. These relationships are examined alongside a more general theme of respect: respect owed to parents, to age, to wisdom, to dukes and to kings. The link between authority and respect is played out between Lear and his daughters, and in the dealings of Kent with Oswald and Cornwall. Loyalty of subjects to masters is also dramatically explored in the pairings of Kent with Lear, Oswald with Goneril, Edmund with Cornwall, Gloucester with both Lear and Cornwall.

A further complex theme emerges which will be developed in the rest of the play: the nature of appearance and reality. In both plots, Shakespeare continues to explore the problem of perception: what is seen and what is hidden, what appears to be true and what are the characters' real intentions. The act contains numerous references to eyes and sight; images of light and darkness also link to this theme and add to the richness of the text and the notions of what can be seen clearly or hidden. Lear and Gloucester fail to see the true natures of their offspring. Edmund, Goneril and Regan all use language to deceive. In contrast, Kent and Edgar use disguise for benign purposes, altering their appearances and accents.

Bound up with the theme of appearance and disguise is the motif of clothing and its casting off. The glory of the court, symbolised in Regan's 'gorgeous' attire, and its artificial order is about to come into sharp contrast with the natural chaos of the storm. The closing of the castle doors against Lear marks a dramatic and symbolic turning point in the play.

Act 3 Scene 1

The purpose of this short scene is to convey information rapidly, to move the plot forward. Kent has been separated from his master. He and the Gentleman officer exchange two kinds of intelligence. The first is news of the king's welfare. The second is military intelligence, delivered and received with caution. Kent reveals that spies in the courts of Albany and Cornwall have reported disagreement between the two dukes and have confirmed rumours that there are plots against Lear. In the Quarto version (see pages 61–2) Kent also reveals that he has received news in Cordelia's letter that she is rallying in defence of her father and that the armies of France will soon arrive. Kent, expecting that the Gentleman will soon meet Cordelia and her forces, gives him a ring. Cordelia will identify the ring as Kent's own, and know that she can trust the messenger. The symbolism is important, for as Kent knows, appearances can deceive: 'I am much more / Than my out-wall' (lines 23–4).

The scene shows that Lear still has strong support and an active intelligence network operating in his favour. But the king is still personally unaware of those facts.

Act 3 Scene 2

> Blow, winds, and crack your cheeks! Rage, blow,
> You cataracts and hurricanoes, spout
> Till you have drenched our steeples, drowned the cocks!
> You sulph'rous and thought-executing fires,
> Vaunt-couriers of oak-cleaving thunderbolts,
> Singe my white head; and thou all-shaking thunder,
> Strike flat the thick rotundity o'th'world,
> Crack nature's moulds, all germens spill at once
> That makes ingrateful man.   *(lines 1–9)*

Lear's famous words of defiance open the scene, emphasising the severity of the storm. Far from shelter, and in spite of being drenched and buffeted, Lear still seeks to command. His speeches challenge any actor, demanding forceful delivery of a passionate and imperative vocabulary: 'Blow', 'crack', 'Rage', 'spout', 'Singe', 'Strike flat', 'spill', 'Rumble', 'spit'. Loud sound effects are not necessary to this scene. The storm comes from Lear himself, a display of his emotional state.

Harley Granville-Barker argues that the storm in itself is 'not dramatically important, only in its effect upon Lear'. He says that the storm must not rival Lear in performance; the actor must take on the role of the old king and 'impersonate' the storm at the same time. As Lear's nine lines above vividly demonstrate, it seems as if he is conjuring up the storm as he speaks.

Lear sees the elements as being in league with his two pernicious daughters, conspiring against him. He is caught up in his own emotional turmoil, and ignores the Fool's advice to give in to his daughters and seek shelter. He pays no heed to the Fool's song about sexual excess and the painful results of irresponsible behaviour because his mind is obsessed with his 'two pernicious daughters'. It is Lear's first taste of real physical suffering, but he seems to accept it with stoical dignity, 'No, I will be the pattern of all patience.' In an eerie echo of Cordelia's acceptance of her lot, Lear resolves:

> I will say nothing. *(line 36)*

Stumbling through the storm, Kent cannot at first make out who are the bedraggled figures before him. The Fool's identification of 'grace and a codpiece; that's a wise man and a fool' is deliberately ambiguous. At an obvious level 'grace' refers to the king and the 'codpiece' to the Fool. However, in this ambiguous statement, the Fool is questioning which of them truly is the wise man and which the fool (just as he had done in Act 1, see pages 12–13). Kent is appalled to find his master so vulnerable to the appalling weather. Yet Lear revels in the ferocity of the storm and its capacity to strike fear into the hearts of sinners:

> Tremble, thou wretch.
> That hast within thee undivulgèd crimes
> Unwhipped of justice. Hide thee, thou bloody hand,
> Thou perjured and thou simular of virtue
> That art incestuous. Caitiff, to pieces shake,
> That under covert and convenient seeming
> Has practised on man's life. *(lines 49–55)*

Lear sees the 'dreadful pudder' of the storm as the gods' judgement upon sinners, and welcomes rather than fears it, believing himself to be 'a man / More sinned against than sinning'. But Kent is more practical. He urges the old king to take shelter in a nearby hut, and intends to have the two daughters take their father back into Gloucester's castle. But Lear ignores him. For the first time in the play he thinks compassionately of others, seeming to take pity on his Fool:

> How dost, my boy? Art cold? *(line 66)*

He agrees to take shelter in the hovel, where there will at least be straw to give them warmth. In such extremity, vile things seem precious. The Fool's song recommends making the best of it. Left alone on stage, as Kent leads Lear to the hovel, the Fool speaks a bizarre prophecy. Some critics have argued his words were written by someone other than Shakespeare, perhaps an actor playing the part of the Fool. The general gist is that after corruption, immorality and unhappiness, Britain ('Albion') will one day return to normality and order. Jacobean audiences might detect in the prophecy a contemporary political issue, perhaps referring to King James I's optimistic vision of a unified Great Britain (see pages 67–8).

Act 3 Scene 3

Whilst Kent finds shelter for Lear, Gloucester ill-advisedly confides in Edmund. Gloucester is worried about the treatment of the king but cannot offer him shelter. Cornwall and Regan have confiscated Gloucester's goods and power and forbidden him to help Lear. Edmund's reaction, 'Most savage and unnatural!', is deliberately ambiguous: whilst he seems to respond as his father expects, he is also ironically describing his own nature and the course of action that he intends to pursue.

Gloucester reveals that he has received a letter from Cordelia. He intends to help Lear in his present distress and support him in the conflict that will inevitably ensue. Gloucester unwittingly trusts this sensitive information to his traitor-son, assuming that Edmund will do as his father bids him. Edmund, however, knows that he can use the latest intelligence as a source of personal gain. Not only his brother's portion, but also the whole of his father's estate and title are within his immediate grasp. Gloucester, like Lear, has now surrendered everything he has to his offspring. His fate is decided.

Act 3 Scene 4

Kent has led Lear and the Fool to the shelter of a hovel. The storm still rages and some productions emphasise the toll that it is taking on the characters. For example, some twentieth-century productions have shown Lear carrying the exhausted Fool in his arms In one production, he wheeled the Fool in a barrow.

Lear refuses to enter the hovel. His physical suffering relieves the anguish in his mind because 'where the greater malady is fixed, / The lesser is scarce felt'. The real storm is in Lear's head, as his thoughts continue to flit between recent events and conversations. The fractured rhythms of his short sentences express the restless movement of his thoughts:

> But I will punish home.
> No, I will weep no more. In such a night
> To shut me out? Pour on, I will endure.
> In such a night as this!   *(lines 16–19)*

Madness remains his greatest fear, but by compassionately persuading the Fool to take shelter in the hovel Lear finds some personal consolation. Urging 'In, boy, go first', he reverses the usual order of things: the king, who always takes precedence, abases himself before the needs of his subject. The irony, which is not lost on Lear, is that by humbling himself, he is spiritually elevated.

For some critics, this episode has striking echoes of Christian teaching (see pages 71–2, 90). Lear's prayer beginning 'Poor naked wretches' suggests that he now acknowledges an important aspect of kingship: a king's duty is not to himself and his immediate family, but to all who are subject to his rule. Living the sheltered and pampered life of a king has, until now, masked for Lear the realities of life. 'Political' critics stress the significance of this moment in the play, which acknowledges that those who are wealthy must have a duty of care towards the poor (see pages 92, 95). Some productions also highlight the episode. For example, the actor-manager William Macready is said to have aimed the speech very deliberately at Queen Victoria in a performance she attended.

The voice of Edgar, disguised as Tom o'Bedlam, is heard as the Fool rushes back out of the hovel. In performance, the disembodied voice may emerge as a cry of despair or as a peal of cackled laughter.

The Fool is terrified, but Lear reacts to Edgar's appearance with two simple questions:

> Didst thou give all to thy daughters? And art thou come to
> this?   *(lines 47–8)*

Suddenly confronted by the sight of another 'poor naked wretch', Lear's thoughts are concerned with what might have brought him so low; it is a sign of his madness that he projects his own misfortunes upon the Bedlam beggar.

What is the meaning of the disjointed exchanges that follow? At the height of a storm a kind of conversation is taking place between an emotionally unbalanced king, a young man pretending to be crazy, a professional fool who fears the storm might send them all mad and a sane man endeavouring to restore sanity to all. Their thoughts appear to range wildly, but express certain preoccupations of the play: filial ingratitude, discarded fathers, poverty, crimes against one's family, and sin, in particular the seven deadly sins. There is a thread of reasoning in Lear's speeches. Edgar's ravings seem unfathomable in comparison, but may suggest an obsession with justice:

> Take heed o'th'foul fiend, obey thy parents, keep thy
> words' justice, swear not, commit not with man's sworn spouse,
> set not thy sweet heart on proud array.   *(lines 73–5)*

In all this jumble of sense and nonsense, the Fool realises that he cannot compete with Edgar whose tags and refrains, such as 'Dauphin, my boy, *cessez!* let him trot by', seem to defy meaning. What is important is Lear's reaction: he takes pity on Tom and his compassion leads him to begin disrobing. Unbuttoning his clothing he wants to strip off the 'lendings', the robes of authority he metaphorically discarded in Act I Scene I when he gave away his lands. His intention seems to become like Poor Tom, 'the thing itself', unclothed and unsophisticated. In his identification with 'Unaccommodated man' he abandons blank verse and adopts the prose speech patterns and the tendency to sexual innuendo of Poor Tom.

In Jacobean times it was a theatrical necessity to remind the audience of times and conditions for the action taking place. Where performances took place in an open theatre in daylight, references to darkness were needed as aural clues to a night-time scene. A visual indicator of night or darkness was the arrival of a torch on stage, as with Gloucester's approach at line 100, described as a 'walking fire'. The difficulties of perception caused by the darkness and torrential rain of the storm are emphasised in the text by repeated requests for people to identify themselves:

KENT   How fares your grace?
LEAR   What's he?
KENT   Who's there? What is't you seek?
GLOUCESTER   What are you there? Your names?   *(lines 111–14)*

Gloucester is acting in direct disobedience of Regan and Goneril who forbade him to succour the old king or to give him shelter. But he cannot ignore the compassion he feels towards Lear. He has for many years been a close counsellor to the king, and like his ruler he is obsessed by filial ingratitude, mistakenly about Edgar:

Our flesh and blood, my lord, is grown so vile,
That it doth hate what gets it.   *(lines 129–30)*

But there is a difference between the two old men. Although Lear may exhibit signs of madness, he at least has begun to understand the part he has played in his own misfortune. Gloucester, on the other hand, in his remarks about ungrateful children, reveals his mistaken beliefs about his sons:

I had a son,
Now outlawed from my blood; he sought my life
But lately, very late. I loved him, friend;
No father his son dearer.   *(lines 150–3)*

Gloucester can see the parallels between Lear's plight and his own, yet he remains self-deluded. Urging stealth, Gloucester directs Lear and the others to more robust shelter. As they all leave, Edgar, in his mad role, speaks three emphatic final lines. Their exact meaning is less important than the general mood they impart. Dark towers, giants and youthful heroes are the very stuff of folk tales, but the threat of death and destruction suggested by these lines is real:

Child Roland to the dark tower came.
His word was still 'Fie, fo, and fum;
I smell the blood of a British man.'   *(lines 166–8)*

Act 3 Scene 5

Edgar's final lines of Scene 4 have set the ominous atmosphere for what is to come. Here, in the 'dark tower' of Gloucester's own castle the bloodiest of deeds are being planned, as Edmund betrays his own father. He shows Cornwall a letter as proof that Gloucester knows of the approach of France's army and of the intention to restore Lear to his kingdom. Cornwall excuses Edmund's disloyalty to his father, citing Gloucester's own 'reprovable badness' as sufficient cause. As reward, he creates Edmund Earl of Gloucester and sends him to arrest his own father. In an aside and then in his promise to Cornwall, Edmund reveals his utter deceitfulness:

> If I find him [Gloucester] comforting the king, it will stuff his
> [Cornwall's] suspicion more fully. – [*To Cornwall*] I will
> persever in my course of loyalty, though the conflict be sore
> between that and my blood.   *(lines 17–19)*

Edmund knows that his father is comforting the king, and his claim to be loyal to his blood is a blatant lie.

Act 3 Scene 6

The outcast king has been led to shelter by Gloucester, who promises him further aid. Gloucester is not yet aware that his title and lands have been passed to Edmund, and Kent's wish that he will be rewarded for his kindness will shortly prove to be bitterly ironic as Gloucester suffers at the hands of Cornwall and Regan.

The mood of the play becomes darker still. Lear is wrapt in his passion and Edgar's commentary on hell and its demons weighs heavily on his mind. He imagines he sees devils with forks, as traditionally represented in doom paintings (representations of the the Last Judgement painted on the walls of churches), exacting revenge on his daughters:

> To have a thousand with red burning spits
> Come hizzing in upon 'em!   *(lines 13–14)*

At this point the Quarto text includes 36 lines not found in Folio. Lear invites the Fool and the madman to join him as judges. In the fantasy trial which follows, Goneril and Regan are put to question, but escape. The 'trial' itself deals with recurring features of the play:

- the folly of trusting flattering behaviour: 'He's mad that trusts in the tameness of a wolf'
- neglect of duty to others: 'Sleepest or wakest thou, jolly shepherd?'
- ill-treatment of parents and the aged: 'she kicked the poor king her father'
- the difference between reality and appearance: 'Cry you mercy' I took you for a joint-stool.'
- the nature of justice itself

This episode is included in most modern productions even though some textual scholars have produced strong evidence that Shakespeare deliberately omitted this business when he revised the play (see page 62). There are compelling theatrical reasons for its inclusion. Not only does it further exemplify Lear's madness, but also it can be acted in ways which present visual echoes of other crucial moments in the play (e.g. the 'love trial' of the opening scene, or the blinding of Gloucester that follows in the next scene).

Throughout Scene 6, the focus is on Lear's madness. Edgar briefly steps out of role, expressing sorrow at what he sees, reminding audiences that whilst he is only 'counterfeiting' madness, Lear is truly deranged. Edgar helps Lear play out the powerful scenes of his imagination. At last, exhausted and hungry, Lear succumbs to sleep, yet there are reversals even here in the final exchange between the king and his Fool:

LEAR We'll go to supper i'th'morning.
FOOL And I'll go to bed at noon.   (lines 40–1)

It is the Fool's parting utterance. After this he appears no more. Some critics hear a definite concluding note in his words, and an admission that he can no longer help Lear. It is early in the play to lose such a vital character and each production must decide how to dismiss the Fool. The 1982 Royal Shakespeare Company's production provided its own drastic solution: the Fool was unwittingly stabbed by Lear.

Gloucester re-enters in a bid to save Lear from certain danger. The urgency and insistence of his advice is demonstrated in the repeated words and phrases of his speech. The lack of a couplet ending to the scene may be Shakespeare's way of suggesting sudden flight. But the Quarto version of the play does not end the scene here. It concludes with a soliloquy spoken by Edgar. Aware that isolation increases suffering, and that fellowship lightens it, Edgar identifies his position with that of Lear, 'He childed as I fathered'. He hopes that he will be reinstated in his father's esteem and that Lear will escape to safety. His course of action must be to bide his time.

Act 3 Scene 7

As the scene opens, Cornwall is making military preparations to counter the invading army of France, and ordering the arrest of Gloucester. Edmund and Goneril are despatched to rouse the Duke of Albany. News is brought that Lear's diminished but loyal retinue has escaped and is on its way to join the French army near Dover.

Gloucester is bundled in and insulted verbally and physically. He is bound like a criminal and when interrogated his answers are taken as lies. 'I am tied to th'stake,' he says, 'and I must stand the course.' Jacobean playgoers would have recognised an image of the helpless baited bear, chained to a post, a common entertainment in the pits near Shakespeare's playhouse. There the bear would be savaged to death by barking and relentless dogs, as Regan and Cornwall behave here. Gloucester has helped Lear to escape their power and in that action has betrayed them.

The usual punishment for a traitor was to be hanged, drawn and quartered and Regan suggests this, but Goneril calls for Gloucester's eyes to be plucked out. In medieval times that punishment was sometimes meted out for the crime of adultery (an offence that Gloucester has committed). It is a vicious sentence, arrived at through a series of repeated references to eyes and their removal:

GONERIL Pluck out his eyes.	*(line 5)*
CORNWALL . . . not fit for your beholding.	*(line 8)*
GLOUCESTER I would not see thy cruel nails	
Pluck out his poor old eyes, . . .	*(lines 55–6)*
But I shall see	

The wingèd vengeance . . .   *lines 64–5)*
CORNWALL See't shalt thou never . . .   *(line 66)*

It was usual Jacobean dramatic practice for extreme violence or murder to take place offstage. The onstage blinding of Gloucester must have been overwhelmingly shocking for Shakespeare's audience, as it remains for audiences today. The staging of this horrific act is critical. In some productions Gloucester is bound to the chair with his back to the audience. At London's Old Vic, Jonathan Miller decided to conduct the blinding offstage. But even if the audience is not in a position to see precisely what is happening, the exertion of violent physical force is evident in Cornwall's words, 'Upon these eyes of thine I'll set my foot.'

As Regan urges her husband to complete the blinding, a servant intervenes. His is the voice of compassion and reason, which sees evil clearly. By Jacobean convention he is lower-born than his master, but he obviously possesses a nobler nature. An audience might experience a moment's hope that this self-elected champion of right can avert further cruelty, but Shakespeare snatches that hope away. Stabbed in the back by Regan, the servant succeeds only in wounding Cornwall, who has strength enough still to complete Gloucester's blinding. The final twist of the knife is not, however, in Gloucester's second eye but, metaphorically, in his heart. As Gloucester calls on Edmund to 'quit this horrid act', Regan gleefully reveals that it was his son who informed upon him. At last, in moments filled with bitter irony, Gloucester sees the truth that was hidden from him whilst he still had eyes.

Cornwall's wound is to prove fatal, but before he leaves the stage his final acts are to turn a helpless blind old man out of doors and deny burial to the virtuous servant.

In the Quarto version of the play, two servants remain on stage to voice their sympathy. They set out to give practical help to Gloucester, one by finding Tom o'Bedlam to act as a guide, the other to get flax and whites of eggs to soothe his bleeding eyes. The inclusion or exclusion of these humanitarian intentions is a crucial dramatic decision (particularly on modern audiences, as this is the usual point to break for an interval). For example, Peter Brook's 1962 production cut the episode. In order to heighten the impression of harshness and cruelty Brook intended to convey, the house lights came up whilst Gloucester still groped blindly about the stage.

Act 3: Critical review

Outlining the action of a single night, the scenes of Act 3 are fast moving. Scenes are alternately set in and out of doors and juxtapose events. For example, in Scenes 4 and 6 Gloucester seeks Lear in the storm and leads him to shelter; a short Scene 5 allows the audience to see Edmund betraying his father within the same timeframe. The audience knows that as he says 'If I find him comforting the king . . .', Gloucester is at the same moment carrying out this act of disobedience.

Fortune's wheel continues to turn for all the characters. The act charts Lear's descent into madness and also maps the path into deeper evil taken by Goneril, Regan, Edmund and Cornwall. Gloucester's journey leads him through moral darkness into a physical blackness so 'dark and comfortless' that there seems to be no destination other than despair. In him the motifs of physical and metaphorical blindness combine. But neither Lear nor Gloucester has yet come to the end of his journey. Lear still hopes to 'go to supper i'th'morning'. His experience of the world has turned topsy-turvy, yet there may remain some promise of restoration.

Edmund, now promoted above his father and bound up with the fates of the new rulers, plans to go higher still. Whilst he rises with the wheel of Fortune, Lear and Gloucester descend. But the suffering of Lear and Gloucester is all too evidently the result of human actions, of power politics, rather than the chance determination of the gods.

The vicious behaviour of Regan and the callous nature of her allies have become fully established. But there has been a break in Albany's exposure to the audience, providing a plausible space of time for the new developments in his role to take place. Cordelia has also been entirely absent from the stage for two acts, although her spiritual presence has grown. The Fool, out-fooled by both his master and by Edgar disguised as Poor Tom, will not appear again.

Act 3 began amidst the fury of a storm, a storm which has raged throughout the night. The act closes with a scene of similar theatrical impact. The blinding of Gloucester provokes its own moral fury, and thunders for justice to be done.

Act 4 Scene 1

The storm has passed. Edgar, still in disguise as Tom o'Bedlam, reflects that from now on his fortunes, and Lear's, will improve. However, the sight of his blinded father touches him deeply and he fears that further suffering lies ahead:

> The worst is not
> So long as we can say 'This is the worst.'   *(lines 27–8)*

Gloucester refuses help from the old man who guides him, saying 'I stumbled when I saw': he realises at last the errors he has made. He recalls the Bedlam beggar, who reminded him of Edgar. The thought prompts him to a bleak assessment of human life. Life is so insignificant and cruelty so arbitrarily meted out, that there is room only for despair:

> As flies to wanton boys are we to th'gods;
> They kill us for their sport.   *(lines 36–7)*

In an ironic twist of fate, Gloucester's blindness has taught him how he misjudged his legitimate son, Edgar. But, like man in a cruel game of the gods, he is helpless, unable to set things to rights. He hints instead at his intention to commit suicide at Dover, led there by Poor Tom. Edgar struggles to sustain his act as Tom o'Bedlam, but decides to keep up the pretence and lead his father away from harm.

Why Edgar does not reveal his true identity to his father has puzzled some audience members. Perhaps he realises that those opposed to Lear will stop at nothing to destroy the king's allies. So his continued deception seems the surest protection for himself and Gloucester. A mad beggar leading a blind man will attract little attention from political enemies. But that is a realistic explanation, and Shakespeare is concerned with a theatrical world of the imagination. In that world, poignancy and dramatic intensity are heightened if the son, unrecognised, leads the sorrowing father who wronged him. Edgar reaches out to Gloucester as a stranger:

> Give me thy arm.
> Poor Tom shall lead thee.   *(lines 73–4)*

Act 4 Scene 2

Oswald tells Goneril that her husband, Albany, has had a change of heart, expressing dislike for her and favouring Lear's cause. Goneril attributes Albany's reluctance to engage in a war with France to cowardice. She proposes to take command of Albany's forces and, with a kiss, she despatches Edmund to carry that message to Cornwall and Regan. Her feelings for Edmund are clear. She is ready to renounce her husband and take Edmund for her consort. Goneril's admiration for Edmund is undisguised, 'To thee a woman's services are due', and her kiss has made her adulterous intention explicit. Edmund leaves only moments before Albany arrives.

Angry that her husband made no effort to greet her arrival, Goneril is sarcastic towards him, 'I have been worth the whistle.' The remark prompts Albany to show his growing contempt for her. The Quarto contains an expanded version of their conversation in which Albany expresses his disgust at how the sisters have behaved towards their father, and at the involvement of Cornwall ('my good brother'):

> Tigers, not daughters, what have you performed?
> A father, and a gracious agèd man,
> Whose reverence even the head-lugged bear would lick,
> Most barbarous, most degenerate, have you madded.
> Could my good brother suffer you to do it?
> A man, a prince, by him so benefited?
> If that the heavens do not their visible spirits
> Send quickly down to tame these vile offences,
> It will come.
> Humanity must perforce prey on itself
> Like monsters of the deep.   (Quarto, *following line 33*)

Goneril retaliates, accusing her husband of cowardice, failure to anticipate threats and casting doubt on his manhood. A messenger who brings news of Cornwall's death and the full horror of the recent events surrounding the blinding of Gloucester interrupts their quarrel. Albany is shocked, yet sees that some kind of justice is at work: 'This shows you are above, / You justicers'. Told that Edmund informed on Gloucester, Albany vows revenge. The messenger has brought Goneril a letter from Regan which excites her jealousy: from now on sexual rivalry will pose a real threat to the British alliance.

A Quarto scene

The Quarto version of *King Lear* includes an extra scene between Scenes 2 and 3. In it, Kent and a Gentleman exchange information. Their conversation reveals that the King of France has returned to his own country, but has left an army in Britain. Cordelia, although moved to tears by news of her father, masters her emotions, remaining 'a queen / Over her passion'. Lear, still mentally deranged, is ashamed and refuses to see Cordelia.

The Gentleman describes Cordelia's reaction to her father's predicament. The delicate imagery of the verse reinforces the gentleness and virtue of Cordelia's character: her smiles and tears are likened to 'Sunshine and rain at once'. Cordelia's response to what her sisters have done has great poignancy. It causes Kent to reflect that the stars, not humans, have created daughters so utterly different from each other:

> It is the stars,
> The stars above us, govern our conditions,
> Else one self mate and make could not beget
> Such different issues.   (Quarto, *lines 32–5*)

Act 4 Scene 3

A dramatic change of pace marks the opening of this scene as the army of France takes the stage with drums beating and flags flying. Cordelia, seen for the first time since Act 1 Scene 1, is at the head of the army. No woman, not even Queen Elizabeth, commanded an army in Shakespeare's time, but Cordelia does. Like her sisters, she has assumed a masculine role for the coming conflict. But the contrast between their nature and Cordelia's is evident in her concern for her father's safety:

> All blest secrets,
> All you unpublished virtues of the earth,
> Spring with my tears; be aidant and remediate
> In the good man's distress.   (*lines 15–18*)

In some productions, Cordelia appears dressed in the ceremonial robes of a queen. In others she wears a simple costume emphasising her humanity and vulnerability. Occasionally she has worn medieval body armour (reminding the audience of Joan of Arc), or modern combat dress. But whatever her costume, she is an active leader giving orders for her father to be found before his madness destroys him.

Cordelia knows that the troops of the British alliance are close by, but shows no fear; her soldiers stand ready for action. Her words 'O dear father, / It is thy business that I go about' echo Christ's words in the temple: 'Wist ye not that I must be about my Father's business?' (Luke 2: 49), and she makes her motives utterly clear:

> No blown ambition doth our arms incite,
> But love, dear love, and our aged father's right.   *(lines 27–8)*

Act 4 Scene 4

This is the fifth consecutive scene in which military intelligence is delivered, moving the plot rapidly forward and propelling all the characters towards Dover. Regan and Oswald exchange news, in a fast-moving prose dialogue. Regan fears that Gloucester's pitiful plight will create enemies, and reports that Edmund is even now seeking to kill him. Discovering that Goneril has written to Edmund but not to her, she becomes suspicious of their liaisons:

> I know your lady does not love her husband.
> I am sure of that; and at her late being here
> She gave strange oeilliads and most speaking looks
> To noble Edmund.   *(lines 25–8)*

Regan subjects Oswald to veiled threats, but he will not surrender Goneril's letter. She therefore orders him to carry her own token to Edmund and urges him to kill Gloucester if their paths cross. The 42 lines of Scene 4 contain much more than military information. They present a catalogue of evils: murder, adultery, duplicity, intrigue, jealousy, suspicion, blackmail, callous self-interest and lust. They also show vividly that relationships between the sisters and their allies are at the point of fracture.

Act 4 Scene 5

Gloucester is intent upon committing suicide, eager to arrive at the top of the cliff from which he plans to jump. Edgar, disguised as Poor Tom, intends to thwart Gloucester's plan and protect him from harm.

He lies to his father, pretending that they are ascending a steep hill, and suggests they are near the cliff top and the sea. Gloucester's comment that Tom's voice sounds different, may echo the audience's perception that Edgar has switched from the mad beggar's prose ranting to the very different rhythm of blank verse. He has almost reached the limit of his role as Tom o'Bedlam and is abandoning his disguise.

The simple exchanges between Edgar and Gloucester at the start of the scene are shot through with ironies and ambiguities. Earlier in the play, Gloucester has been deceived by Edmund for malign purposes. Now Edgar will deceive him, but with benign intentions. Edgar's remarkable description of an imagined Dover cliff emphasises the dizzy heights to which he claims to have led Gloucester. In a sentence that combines onomatopoeia and assonance, Edgar gives a convincing reason why Gloucester might not be able to hear the sea crashing below:

> The murmuring surge,
> That on th'unnumbered idle pebble chafes,
> Cannot be heard so high.   *(lines 20–2)*

Playing along with Gloucester's suicidal intention, Edgar tricks him into believing that he stands on the very brink of the cliff, then pretends to leave him there. He reassures the audience in an aside:

> Why I do trifle thus with his despair
> Is done to cure it.   *(lines 33–4)*

Gloucester rewards his guide, kneels in a valedictory speech and asks a blessing for Edgar. Once he is certain that no one will prevent his fall, he throws himself forward. Theatrically, this is one of the most stunning scenes of the play. It needs no scenery, only an empty, level stage. Shakespeare's language uses the power of suggestion to create the illusions of height and seascape. It works upon the imaginations of Gloucester and the audience alike. In Victorian times, huge painted backdrops of Dover cliff dominated the scene, but in the twentieth and twenty-first centuries productions have returned to the flat empty stage of Shakespeare's own theatre. Such simple staging produces dazzling theatre, charged with dramatic irony. Gloucester throws himself forward, falling upon a flat stage and Edgar breaks the spell of illusion:

> Had he been where he thought,
> By this had thought been past. *(lines 44–5)*

Gloucester is never made aware of what has happened, and Edgar tricks him into believing another fantastical account. He takes on a new identity and continues the deception of the fall. He pretends not to notice Gloucester's blindness, and suggests that he was led to his suicide by a horned demon, an image plucked from medieval doom paintings on church walls. Tom o'Bedlam in his fiendish disguise has fled and Gloucester's preservation has been miraculous:

> He had a thousand noses,
> Horns whelked and waved like the enragèd sea.
> It was some fiend. Therefore, thou happy father,
> Think that the clearest gods, who make them honours
> Of men's impossibilities, have preserved thee. *(lines 70–4)*

Now the two plot lines merge and interweave: Lear's story and Gloucester's. Lear arrives, variously described in different editions of the play as 'mad' or 'dressed fantastically'. In most productions he wears flowers and weeds (mentioned by Cordelia in Act 4 Scene 3, lines 3–6). His mind flits and wanders between ideas and images. Seemingly disconnected and nonsensical, they embody some of the play's major preoccupations: kingship, authority and respect, deceptive appearances, mortality, adultery and the nature of justice.

Lear's first utterance reveals that his mind is occupied with kingship and authority: 'No, they cannot touch me for crying. I am the king himself.' Although he does not wear the robes of a king, he believes he still retains authority, because kings are born not made: 'Nature's above art in that respect.' The Jacobean audience would recognise the reference here to the doctrine of the divine right of kings, in which James I fervently believed (see page 66).

Lear's mind leaps now from the theme of rightful authority to his own need to counter the attack from Goneril and Regan's forces on his kingship. He imagines that he is assembling an army, paying incentives to longbow-men and halberdiers, and encouraging their military skills:

> There's your press-money [the king's shilling paid to recruits].
> That fellow handles his bow like a crow-keeper. Draw me a
> clothier's yard [the full stretch of the longbow] . . .
> Bring up the brown bills [halberdiers]. O well flown bird:
> i'th'clout, i'th'clout! [an arrow hits the centre of the target]
> *(Lines 85–90)*

Something in Gloucester's appearance reminds Lear of Goneril. Deep in his anguish, he remembers how his disrespectful daughters used false loyalty, flattery and empty promises to deceive him:

> They flattered me like a dog and told me I had the white hairs
> in my beard ere the black ones were there. To say 'ay' and 'no'
> to everything that I said 'ay' and 'no' to was no good divinity.
> *(lines 94–7)*

Lear recalls the storm and how, powerless against it, he came to recognise his own frailty and mortality, to see that although a king, he was only a man, subject like all others to human frailty:

> When the rain came to wet me once and the wind to make me
> chatter, when the thunder would not peace at my bidding,
> there I found 'em, there I smelt 'em out. Go to, they are not
> men o'their words. They told me I was everything; 'tis a lie, I
> am not ague-proof. *(lines 97–101)*

Reminded by Gloucester that he is still the king, Lear resumes an air of authority: 'Ay, every inch a king.' However, perhaps prompted by the sight of Gloucester's bandaged eyes, his fevered thoughts turn to the punishment for adultery and he embarks upon an impassioned rant about sexual behaviour. He imagines all of nature to be engaged in sex: 'Let copulation thrive'. He increasingly expresses disgust as he thinks of his own cruel daughters, 'Got 'tween the lawful sheets', and of the lustful nature of even the most virtuous-seeming woman. In his tortured vision, the female genitals become the source of the burning diseases of infected sex:

> There's hell, there's darkness, there is the sulphurous pit,
> burning, scalding, stench, consumption. *(lines 124–5)*

Moved by Lear's plight, Gloucester tries to discover whether the king recognises him. The poignancy of the conversation between the two men increases; it is full of heart-aching references to eyes and seeing and with wordplay on perception, culminating in Gloucester's 'I see it feelingly.' Lear reacts forcefully. Sight is not, he says, the only sense through which man understands the nature of things: 'look with thine ears'. Lear gives a series of examples to show how deceptive appearances can make justice hard to administer (see pages 69–71). The language style and topsy-turvy imagery strongly resemble the riddles and questions of his absent Fool:

> See how yon justice rails upon yon simple thief. Hark in thine
> ear: change places, and handy-dandy, which is the justice,
> which is the thief? *(lines 145–7)*

In a world where respectability and hypocrisy go hand in hand to punish poverty, Lear has come to realise that either all must be punished or all pardoned: 'None does offend, none, I say none.'

Lear's order to remove his boots, whether they are real or imaginary, is a further step in Lear's symbolic disrobing. In Act 1 he cast away his crown, surrendering the rule of his realm to others. In Act 3 he threw off his 'Robes and furred gowns' at the height of the storm, renouncing his kingly finery and becoming an ordinary man. Now Lear goes barefoot, like a child or a beggar. In this humble state he offers his dearest sense, eyesight, to Gloucester, and preaches patience through suffering. Lear has learnt humility and patience for himself and shows gentleness towards Gloucester. But Lear's wandering thoughts return to practical matters. To survive on 'this great stage of fools', Lear needs to defend himself. He considers the preparations and stealth he must use to approach his enemies:

> It were a delicate stratagem to shoe
> A troop of horse with felt. I'll put't in proof,
> And when I have stol'n upon these son-in-laws,
> Then kill, kill, kill, kill, kill, kill! *(lines 176–9)*

With his mind fixed on plans for bloodshed, Lear assumes that Cordelia's troops have come to arrest him. He runs from them, like a child in a game of tag. The Gentleman officer's comment expresses the depths to which Lear has sunk:

A sight most pitiful in the meanest wretch,
Past speaking of in a king. *(lines 195–6)*

Edgar's request for reports of the war's progress takes the scene into its final movement. With the armies closing in, Gloucester must be taken to safety but, even now, Edgar does not reveal his identity to his father. Their way is suddenly barred by the arrival of Oswald, who sees his opportunity for self-advancement in the 'proclaimed prize' of Gloucester. He draws his sword to kill the old man, and Gloucester seems to welcome the prospect of death. But Edgar steps in to defend his father.

Edgar assumes a new accent, a rural style of speech. Perhaps Shakespeare's intention in making this switch was to have Oswald killed by a man of seemingly lower social status. Or Edgar may be mocking Oswald for adopting a fancy fencing style, when he is armed only with a stick ('ballow'). Oswald does not recognise Edgar, who mortally wounds him. Close to death, Oswald offers his purse to Edgar as incentive to bury him and deliver the letter he carries to Edmund.

Out of Gloucester's hearing, Edgar breaks open the letter. In it Goneril reveals her desire for Edmund, her loathing for Albany, and her wish that Edmund should kill her husband. Edgar decides at once that he must reveal the contents of the letter to Albany. He sets out to bury Oswald's body, leaving Gloucester to reflect that he could forget his own sorrows if only he were mad like Lear:

The king is mad. How stiff is my vile sense
That I stand up and have ingenious feeling
Of my huge sorrows! Better I were distract
So should my thoughts be severed from my griefs
(lines 267–70)

The ominous sound of drums in the distance hastens Edgar to take his father's hand. He hopes to lead Gloucester to a place of safety.

Act 4 Scene 6

Shakespeare follows the high drama of Scene 5 with a contrastingly quiet scene. A line in the Quarto text suggests that this particular scene, in which Kent, Cordelia and Lear are united, would be accompanied by soft music. It is in character for Kent to admit to Cordelia that he needs no reward for his services to Lear, other than to be recognised. For the moment, however, he considers it best to remain disguised. Cordelia prays that her father's mental health will be restored and agrees to have him woken from his healing sleep. Lear is brought on to the stage.

The symbolism of Lear's entrance is striking. Lear has been re-clothed whilst sleeping and no longer wears 'fantastical weeds'. Sometimes he is carried onto the stage on a royal throne, dressed in ceremonial robes. Sometimes his clothes, and the chair on which he is carried, are simple, more appropriate to a military camp than a royal court. Cordelia bestows a kiss of restoration upon her father, but it does not have an immediate fairy-tale effect. Her words express both her compassion and the ordeal through which Lear has passed, experiencing suffering and degradation:

> Was this a face
> To be opposed against the warring winds?
> Mine enemy's dog,
> Though he had bit me, should have stood that night
> Against my fire. And wast thou fain, poor father,
> To hovel thee with swine and rogues forlorn
> In short and musty straw?   (lines 31–7)

Lear takes a while to revive, and when he does, he uses a cosmic image that combines mythology of earth, heaven and hell (see page 77):

> You do me wrong to take me out o'th'grave.
> Thou art a soul in bliss, but I am bound
> Upon a wheel of fire, that mine own tears
> Do scald like molten lead.   (lines 42–5)

Cordelia kneels to ask her father's blessing. Lear attempts to do the same, although she tries to prevent him. When Lear kneels to

Cordelia, it contrasts dramatically in tone and feeling with the earlier scene when Lear knelt before Regan (Act 2 Scene 4, line 146). In both instances, he speaks of his advanced age, mockingly to Regan in the earlier scene ('Age is unnecessary: on my knees I beg / That you'll vouchsafe me raiment, bed, and food', lines 147–8), but now to Cordelia he speaks simply and genuinely:

> Pray do not mock me:
> I am a very foolish, fond old man,
> Fourscore and upward,
> Not an hour more nor less; and to deal plainly,
> I fear I am not in my perfect mind.   *(lines 56–60)*

Lear's madness has evaporated. He sees plainly, recognising himself and others, although not yet ready to claim certainty about anything. Cordelia reassures him, and her wet tears are the physical proof that he can truly believe what he sees before him. His submission to Cordelia is total as he acknowledges his wrongs against her:

> If you have poison for me, I will drink it.
> I know you do not love me; for your sisters
> Have, as I do remember, done me wrong.
> You have some cause; they have not.   *(lines 70–3)*

Cordelia's reply expresses full and absolute forgiveness: 'No cause, no cause.' Here, in one of the gentlest moments of the play, Cordelia offers her father her arm, in a gesture reminiscent of Lear's to his Fool and Edgar's to Gloucester. When Lear asks Cordelia to forget and forgive, hope, reconciliation and regeneration seem very close, but so too does the rumble of the drums.

Act 4: Critical review

During Act 4, all the characters make their way to Dover, where the final events of the play will take place, and the two plots merge. Until now, the events of the Lear plot and the Gloucester plot have remained largely separate with only a few chance meetings and crossovers, such as when Edgar, exiled from his inheritance, joins the king's dishevelled retinue. Following the blinding of Gloucester, events in one plot influence more directly events in the other, and they interweave fully in Scene 5 when Lear and Gloucester meet.

The act is strongly structured. In Scenes 1 and 5, Edgar and Gloucester take the greater parts. These two scenes create a frame for a set of three cameo scenes. In Scene 2, Goneril makes her wishes and intentions known. Her lust for Edmund is evident. In Scene 4, Regan does the same, and once again lust for Edmund motivates the sisters' rivalry. These two scenes stand as contrasts on either side of Scene 3, where Cordelia appears as a loving daughter, queen and potential redeemer of her father.

Little is seen of Lear himself in the first four scenes, although others follow his progress closely, and he is the subject of the dialogue in Scene 3. Scene 5 marks his entry as a changed man, yet still vulnerable as he runs from those who seek him. In Scene 6 he is the central focus, penitent, his sanity regained.

Act 4 combines and intensifies themes which have closely linked both plots. Justice and fortune have shaped each individual's destiny. Casting off clothing and maintaining disguise, deception, trust and loyalty have figured prominently. Madness, sight and blindness, recognition and revelation are dramatically explored, most poignantly in Scene 5. All might be interpreted as aspects of a favourite theme of Shakespeare's: the nature of appearance and reality.

At the end of the act, with Lear and Cordelia reunited, the king's restoration might seem imminent. Gloucester and Edgar are almost reconciled. The letter in Edgar's possession provides the means for defeating the evil personified in Edmund, Goneril and Regan. There appears to be hope for a good and just ending, but Act 5 will dramatise a very different reality.

Act 5 Scene 1

Dramatic tension increases as the noise and splendour of drum and colours (military flags) introduce the final act. There is a note of uncertainty in the conversation between Edmund and Regan. Edmund worries that Albany's changeable moods mean he may not support their cause. Regan thinks Oswald has 'miscarried': the audience knows the reason why Goneril's messenger has not appeared. The sisters' sexual rivalry over Edmund is evident as Regan questions him directly about whether he has slept with Goneril, delivering the ominous threat, 'I never shall endure her.' Her words lend dramatic irony to Albany's greeting, 'Our very loving sister'.

The Quarto includes extra lines in which Goneril declares 'I had rather lose the battle than that sister / Should loosen him and me' (after line 14). It also has Albany express misgivings about engaging in the war (at line 18), to which Edmund makes a curt, sarcastic reply, 'Sir, you speak nobly'.

The rivalry between the sisters surfaces directly as Goneril refuses to accompany her sister. Her aside, 'O ho, I know the riddle', reveals the distrust between them. Neither will allow the other to be alone for a moment in Edmund's presence.

Edgar, disguised as a peasant, hands Albany the letter which will reveal the intimacy between Goneril and Edmund. He asks Albany to summon a champion if he should have success in battle, and declares he will produce a champion in response to the trumpet call. Whether Albany has time to read the letter before Edmund reappears is left open for every production to decide, but Edmund urges swift action and Albany leaves to prepare his troops.

Edmund's soliloquy reveals the character traits of duplicity and ruthless self-seeking that have brought him so close to power. He discloses that he has made promises to both Goneril and Regan. He realises that when he makes his choice between them, one must die. He also intends ill towards Albany, planning to make use of his army in the battle, then have Goneril devise the manner of Albany's death, 'Let her who would be rid of him devise / His speedy taking off'. Chillingly, he also intends the death of Lear and Cordelia. For self-preservation he needs to ensure that they are both destroyed:

> for my state
> Stands on me to defend, not to debate   *(lines 57–8)*

Act 5 Scene 2

The signal for the start of battle is given, 'Alarum within.' Cordelia, with Lear at her side, leads her army across the stage. The sounds of the battle explode as Edgar sets Gloucester down in a safe spot. He hopes and expects that Cordelia's army may win: 'If ever I return to you again / I'll bring you comfort.' The interval between Edgar's departure and return may be brief, but the striking stage image is that of an old, blind, helpless man. Gloucester may do as Edgar suggests and pray silently, but however he behaves it is a fraught moment in which Gloucester and the audience hear the distant sounds of battle.

The retreat is sounded and Edgar brings bad news. Lear and Cordelia have been defeated and taken captive. Edgar urges flight, but Gloucester sinks into despair: 'a man may rot even here'. His despondency is countered by Edgar's stoical call for patience and endurance:

> What, in ill thoughts again? Men must endure
> Their going hence even as their coming hither:
> Ripeness is all. *(lines 9–11)*

Act 5 Scene 3

Edmund's triumphant entrance opens the final scene. It signals his rise to the top of Fortune's wheel. He orders that Lear and Cordelia be sent to prison. Although they are prisoners, Lear and Cordelia are happy to be reunited. They talk together, unperturbed by the gaze of Edmund and the soldiers. Cordelia is sanguine in her response to defeat. Others with well-intentioned aims have also met unlucky ends, 'We are not the first / Who with best meaning have incurred the worst.' She selflessly assures her father that her worries are for him alone:

> For thee, oppressèd king, I am cast down,
> Myself could else outfrown false fortune's frown. *(lines 5–6)*

Lear emphatically rejects the suggestion that he and Cordelia should see Goneril and Regan, 'No, no, no, no!' He wishes to go straight to prison where he can be alone with Cordelia and enjoy their reconciliation, 'like birds i'th'cage'. With an echo of the scene where he wakes from his madness (Act 4 Scene 6), Lear imagines the ways

in which they will endure their time in prison. He will 'kneel down /
And ask of thee forgiveness'. Sometimes both Lear and Cordelia kneel
together at this moment, making it even more personal and intimate,
and displaying their complete absorption with one another.

Lear proposes that he and Cordelia will engage in simple, innocent
pastimes, 'And pray, and sing, and tell old tales, and laugh / At gilded
butterflies'. The image of the bright butterflies leads Lear to think of
the golden finery of courtiers. He imagines hearing the gossip from
court and discovering who the new favourites are, 'who's in, who's
out'. Lear says that he and Cordelia will be like 'God's spies', knowing
all the secrets, yet keeping aloof. Their walled prison will act as a
defence, protecting them from the fickle nature of political wrangling.
In prison they will outlast those

> packs and sects of great ones
> That ebb and flow by th'moon   *(lines 18–19)*

The image is of the tides: the height and depth of the tide and its daily
ebbing and flowing is governed by the moon, which is always
changing. The Jacobeans characterised the moon as inconstant and
fickle, and Shakespeare uses it and its influence on the tides here to
reflect the instability of the royal court under new leadership. Lear
thinks that he and Cordelia, imprisoned, will enjoy immunity from
this political circus, but Edmund's curt order betrays a cruel reality:
'Take them away.'

Lear tells Cordelia that the gods themselves look kindly upon the
sacrifices they have made: she in hazarding all to assist her ageing
father, he in all the suffering he has endured. The lines are poignantly
prophetic too, for Cordelia's sacrifice is not yet complete. Lear cannot
believe his good fortune in winning back his daughter. He cries: 'Have
I caught thee?', and reassures her that only a cataclysmic event, 'a
brand from heaven', can separate them now. As they are hustled away
to prison, Cordelia's tears make her father defiant against their
enemies:

> Wipe thine eyes.
> The goodyears shall devour them, flesh and fell,
> Ere they shall make us weep. We'll see 'em starved first.
> *(lines 23–5)*

Edmund now puts into action his intention to send Lear and Cordelia to their deaths, and despatches an officer to kill them. Moments later Albany, Regan and Goneril arrive. Albany acknowledges Edmund's bravery in battle but is curtly polite in his demand that Lear and Cordelia are delivered to him. Edmund reasons that by sending them to prison he is preventing uprisings in support of Lear. The power struggle between them is conducted in formal speeches, each man beginning with apparent deference ('Sir') which thinly disguises their animosity.

When Albany seeks to put Edmund in his place, reminding him that he is a subject, not an equal, Regan upholds his status. Her words provoke an angry retort from Goneril. A squabble ensues between the sisters, and Regan, although beginning to fall sick, declares her intention to marry Edmund. She uses words of a military surrender:

> General,
> Take thou my soldiers, prisoners, patrimony.
> Dispose of them, of me; the walls is thine.
> Witness the world that I create thee here
> My lord and master.   *(lines 68–72)*

Knowing of his wife's lustful behaviour from the intercepted letter, Albany allows all three to implicate themselves before attempting to arrest Edmund for treason and Goneril for collaboration. He switches to using familiar ('thee', 'thy') rather than respectful pronouns (you, your) as he addresses Edmund. His sarcasm displays contempt for Regan too as he declares his wife has prior claim to Edmund. In turn Goneril mocks her husband's theatricality, 'An interlude!' But Albany sustains his superior moral and social position, throwing down his glove as a direct challenge to Edmund. The challenge is to a duel, or trial by combat. By now Regan has fallen very ill, but with the excitement of the challenge her distress is barely noted, except by the delighted Goneril. She hints that the cause of Regan's sickness is poison ('medicine').

Edmund attempts to call Albany's bluff. Rather than accept the challenge, for he does not pick up the glove, he throws down his own. The arrogance of this is not lost on Albany, but the duke has two advantages: a champion in waiting and a proclamation already prepared to hand to the Herald. Albany reminds Edmund that he lacks military support, and, as the sick Regan is escorted to Albany's tent, the champion is summoned by a trumpet call. Neither the first nor the second trumpet call is answered, but on the third Edgar's trumpet is heard in reply. Edgar appears armed and helmeted, an unrecognised and sinister figure. His reply to the Herald's questions obliquely offers clues to his identity:

> Know, my name is lost,
> By treason's tooth bare-gnawn and canker-bit.
> Yet am I noble as the adversary
> I come to cope.   *(lines 111–14)*

Edmund disdains to follow the accepted tradition that gives him the right to know his opponent's status. For him it is enough that the newcomer 'looks so fair and warlike' and his manner of speech 'of breeding breathes'. He will not delay the fight over niceties. How the fight is staged varies vastly from production to production: sometimes it is highly stylised, evidently following the formal rules of chivalry, at other times it is savage, realistic and dirty. When Edmund falls, Albany orders a reprieve. Edmund is worth more to him alive for the moment, although he is mortally wounded. Goneril swiftly claims that the fight is unfair, as the proper procedure has not been followed. Albany vehemently silences her:

> Shut your mouth, dame,
> Or with this paper shall I stop it.   *(lines 144–5)*

He orders that Edmund reads the letter which reveals Goneril's plot. Goneril attempts to snatch the letter away, and as she sweeps out declares, as her father had done (Act 4 Scene 5, line 83), that her royalty places her above judgement:

> the laws are mine, not thine.
> Who can arraign me for't?   *(lines 148–9)*

Faced with the incriminating letter, Edmund admits his guilt. He asks to know the identity of his opponent, and in the spirit of chivalry, forgives him. Edgar reveals himself, and although he offers good will ('charity') he cannot resist the opportunity to moralise on the hard justice which made Edmund the 'instrument' by which Gloucester answered for his adultery:

> The gods are just, and of our pleasant vices
> Make instruments to plague us.
> The dark and vicious place where thee he got
> Cost him his eyes.   *(lines 160–3)*

Edmund agrees, 'The wheel is come full circle': his fortune, once so high, has now brought him to the point of death. Albany greets Edgar, eager to know his story. Edgar tells of the death of Gloucester, and his own regret that he did not ask his father's blessing in time. Edmund is 'moved' by his brother's tale, but before he can do the 'good' he promises, events rapidly intervene. A Gentleman brings the bloody knife that Goneril has used to commit suicide, after confessing that she poisoned Regan. Albany orders that the bodies of the two sisters should be brought out. He is instantly obeyed, and the bodies remain on stage, serving as a visual reminder of death, throughout the remaining action.

Kent has come to pay his respects to Lear and is surprised not to find him. Shocked by his own negligence, Albany cries 'Great thing of us forgot!' He demands Edmund to tell him where Lear and Cordelia are and, panting for life and struggling for words, Edmund acts uncharacteristically:

> Some good I mean to do,
> Despite of mine own nature. Quickly send –
> Be brief in it – to th'castle; for my writ
> Is on the life of Lear and on Cordelia.   *(lines 217–20)*

Edmund reveals the full treachery of the plan he and Goneril had hatched, to make Cordelia's death seem like suicide. As he is carried off, Lear enters with Cordelia dead in his arms. Lear's agony is expressed in his anguished repetition:

> Howl, howl, howl, howl!   *(line 231)*

Some critics have seen this stage picture as resembling a *pietà*, in which Christ's body, taken down from the cross, is cradled in His mother's arms. Most Jacobeans would have known the image from church paintings and understood it as a symbol of redemption. Whether Shakespeare intended the audience to make this connection or not, it is a picture of desperate grief. Lear calls for all the 'men of stones' who watch to weep with him so that their lamentation might crack the sky itself ('heaven's vault'). He plays out a forlorn charade, checking for signs of life in Cordelia, laying down her body and calling for a looking glass, 'If that her breath will mist or stain the stone, / Why then she lives'.

Kent, Edgar and Albany comment on the tragic sight. Kent asks if it is 'the promised end' of the Day of Judgement, and Edgar also wonders if this will be how doomsday will look, the 'image of that horror'. Albany's 'Fall and cease' seems to call to the heavens for a swift ending to the painful sight, or to all human suffering.

Lear makes a second test for faint breathing, placing a feather near to Cordelia's lips: 'This feather stirs, she lives'. The simplicity of the words is deceptive. They might mean that Lear thinks he sees the feather stir, and that Cordelia is alive and breathing. Or the words might ask those nearby to agree that if this feather stirs, it will be a sign that she still lives. The ambiguity of the sentence sums up Lear's heart-breaking desire and hope that Cordelia lives in spite of the evidence before him. He cannot resign himself to accepting her death, and cannot rule out the possibility that:

> if it be so,
> It is a chance which does redeem all sorrows
> That ever I have felt   *(lines 239–41)*

Kent chooses this harrowing moment to ask Lear for recognition and to offer help. Lear dismisses him, suggesting that it is the interference of others that has brought about Cordelia's death. He is still reluctant to accept it, gently calling her back from death and seeming to hear her speak:

> Cordelia, Cordelia, stay a little. Ha?
> What is't thou sayst?   *(lines 245–6)*

It is as if Lear answers a question she has asked when he says 'I killed the slave that was a-hanging thee.' Although strong enough to kill a man, Lear admits that his age robs him of his previous might, and has faded his eyesight. But he recognises Kent who stands before him, although for Kent this is not enough. He wants Lear to realise that in his role as Caius he has remained loyally at his side throughout his sufferings. Lear cannot make the connection; for him Caius may have been a good fellow but 'He's dead and rotten'. Kent tries to resume his role as Lear's adviser, pointing out the bodies of the elder daughters, but their deaths do not matter to the old king, who has thoughts only for Cordelia.

News of Edmund's death arrives, but is dismissed by Albany as an irrelevance. Albany declares he will restore Lear to his throne, resigning his own right to rule. He returns to Edgar and Kent their lands and titles, and intends to see that justice is done as friends 'taste / The wages of their virtue', and foes 'The cup of their deservings'. But he is unable to complete the ceremony he has begun. He refocuses attention on Lear and Cordelia: 'O see, see!'

Lear seems to be in the middle of a thought: 'And my poor fool is hanged.' He is almost certainly thinking of Cordelia, but his words bring to mind the Fool, who was also dear to the old king. Lear rages at the injustice of Cordelia's death:

> Why should a dog, a horse, a rat have life,
> And thou no breath at all? Thou'lt come no more,
> Never, never, never, never, never.
> Pray you, undo this button. Thank you, sir.
> Do you see this? Look on her! Look, her lips.
> Look there, look there. *(lines 280–5)*

Does he die thinking he sees that Cordelia lives? Every reader and audience member must make their own decision. Edgar tries to revive Lear, but Kent stops him, knowing that his master had reached the limit of his suffering and was ready for death:

EDGAR   He faints. My lord, my lord!
KENT Break, heart, I prithee break.
EDGAR   Look up, my lord.
KENT Vex not his ghost. O, let him pass. He hates him
          That would upon the rack of this tough world
          Stretch him out longer. *(lines 285–9)*

Albany tries to hand the rule of the kingdom jointly to Edgar and Kent, but Kent will not accept, forecasting he will shortly join Lear in death:

> I have a journey, sir, shortly to go:
> My master calls me; I must not say no.   *(lines 295–6)*

Edgar takes on the heavy responsibility alone, receiving his new duty with caution and sadness. His words that close the play show he is aware of the demands his new position of authority will make upon him: 'we must obey'. He pledges that under his rule integrity will replace flattery and deceit. Edgar has witnessed and learnt from the sufferings of his elders, and he doubts that he and his contemporaries can match their experience:

> The weight of this sad time we must obey,
> Speak what we feel, not what we ought to say.
> The oldest hath borne most; we that are young
> Shall never see so much, nor live so long.   *(lines 297–300)*

Act 5: Critical review

Scene 1 makes evident the rivalry of Goneril and Regan for Edmund's sexual favours, but his soliloquy reveals a cynical indifference: either sister will do so long as his political ambitions are fulfilled. In Scene 2, Cordelia's army is defeated offstage, and Edgar urges his blinded father to endure his suffering patiently. Both scenes are short precursors to the denouement of Scene 3.

Traditionally, in the final act of a play, audiences expect the events to be wound up, with justice done and right restored. In *King Lear*, Shakespeare denies the audience the comfort and reassurance of such an ending. Lear and Cordelia appear as prisoners, and Edmund orders their murder. Cordelia is hanged, but Lear slays the murderer and in the final harrowing episode appears with Cordelia dead in his arms. He hopes against hope that she lives, and dies urging the onstage audience to look on her lips, as though he believes she might be about to speak: 'Look there, look there.'

Critical opinion is divided as to whether the final scene is hopeful or nihilistic. There seem to be two problems, one minor and one major. The minor problem is Edgar's accession. Although young and virtuous, he lacks the authority and presence of a confident leader. His insistence that we must 'Speak what we feel, not what we ought to say' suggests that he has learnt little from experience: Cordelia, who did exactly that, lies dead before him.

Cordelia's death presents the major problem. Why should such an innocent character die? It seems counter to any idea of justice, human or divine. Many actors, critics and audiences have found the bleakness of this ending too devastating and desolate to accept. For 150 years, a happy ending was substituted (see pages 84, 98–9) in which Cordelia lived and even ruled with Edgar at her side. But this is not the ending that Shakespeare intended. His bleak closure stuns the characters on stage and the audience. The Folio includes a stage direction '*Exeunt with a dead march*', suggesting that the play ends in a solemn funeral procession. Modern productions do not often show that formal ritual, choosing to emphasise stillness and silence in a frozen tableau of the living and the dead.

Contexts

This section identifies the contexts from which *King Lear* emerged: the wide range of different influences that fostered the creativity of Shakespeare as he wrote the play. These contexts ensured that *King Lear* engaged with the familiar knowledge, assumptions, beliefs and values of Jacobean England.

What did Shakespeare write?

Sometime during 1605 or 1606, William Shakespeare, already an established and successful playwright, wrote *King Lear*. What was the play that Shakespeare wrote and his audiences heard? No one knows for certain because his original script has not survived, nor have any handwritten amendments he might subsequently have made. Three published versions of the play exist, two Quartos and a Folio version. Quarto and folio refer to the size of the paper used for printing. Quarto is about the size of this book you are reading, Folio is over twice the size.

The first Quarto edition of the play was published in 1608, titled *The True Chronicle History of the Life and Death of King Lear*. It is sometimes known as the Pied Bull Quarto, named after the sign advertising a printer's workshop. It is an inaccurately printed edition, full of mistakes and inconsistent punctuation. The second Quarto edition appeared in 1619, just three years after Shakespeare died. It carried the same title and date (1608) and is basically a reprint of the first Quarto. When scholars speak of 'the Quarto', they are referring to the 1608 version.

The First Folio, a collection of 36 plays, was published in 1623, seven years after Shakespeare's death. Here, the play is titled *The Tragedie of King Lear*, and it is different from the Quarto in many respects:

- It includes about 100 new lines, not found in the Quarto.
- It cuts around 300 lines that appear in the Quarto.
- Some lines are given to different speakers.

Some differences between the Quarto and the Folio are minor, but others change the sense of lines, affect the action and mood and alter characterisation. To give only two examples, the mock trial of Goneril and Regan only appears in the Quarto, and in the Folio no servants come to the aid of Gloucester after he has been blinded.

There are, then, two clearly different versions of *King Lear* and the debate continues over which version more closely resembles the play Shakespeare intended to be acted. Many scholars argue that the Quarto represents Shakespeare's first version of the play, and the Folio *King Lear* is the result of his revision in the light of experience of performance and censorship. But because no copy written in the dramatist's own hand exists, arguments over the two versions still continue. Nonetheless, the comments of Stanley Wells are helpful:

> The reader who wishes to come closest to Shakespeare in the heat of original composition will prefer the Quarto-based version; the reader who is more interested in the theatrical realization of the text by the company of players of which Shakespeare was a member will prefer the Folio. And the reader who is interested in the way the process of rehearsal and production may transmute a text will wish to compare the two.

Some modern editions use the Quarto version; others use the Folio. Most include the differing passages in appendices for comparison. Some editions are 'conflations', combining Quarto and Folio versions, but many critics argue against this practice. The edition of the play you are using will certainly vary in many minor respects from other editions. That is because every editor of the play makes a multitude of different judgements about such matters as spelling, punctuation, stage directions, scene locations and other features. It is important that you read any introductory material in your edition to find out whether you are reading a text based on the Quarto, the Folio or a conflation. This Guide follows the New Cambridge edition of the play (also used in Cambridge School Shakespeare) which is based on the First Folio, but which includes Quarto extracts for comparison.

What did Shakespeare read?
Shakespeare's genius lay in his ability to transform what he read into gripping drama. This section is therefore about the influence of genre: the literary and dramatic contexts of *King Lear*. It identifies the stories

and dramatic conventions that fired Shakespeare's imagination as he wrote *King Lear*.

Stories of King Lear existed for over 400 years before Shakespeare's time. The oldest known version is the Latin text *Historia Regum Britanniae*. Its author, Geoffrey of Monmouth, chronicles the lives and exploits of the kings of Britain up to the time of his writing in 1136. Geoffrey was an imaginative writer and much of what he wrote is not historically accurate. There are no known Elizabethan translations of Monmouth's history, but Shakespeare may have read it in the original Latin, or in accounts made by more recent writers.

One of these accounts appeared in Ralph Holinshed's *Chronicles of England, Scotland and Ireland* (1577) which Shakespeare had already used extensively as source material for a number of his plays. Other books which retold the Lear story were known to Shakespeare: *The Mirror for Magistrates* (1574), and Edmund Spenser's *The Faerie Queene* (1589). But whatever Shakespeare took from his reading, he never slavishly copied his models, but instead adapted his source materials to create thrilling drama. For instance, in all the versions mentioned, Cordelia commits suicide, but Shakespeare replaces her suicide with execution.

Shakespeare was not the only playwright to dramatise the story of King Lear. In 1605 a play entitled *The True Chronicle History of Leir King of England and His Three Daughters* was published anonymously. It took the simple plot line from the old story but included no deaths, and restored Leir to his throne. Shakespeare certainly knew of this play (some scholars claim he acted in it) because it had been around at least since 1594. What is not certain is whether the play was printed in 1605 due to a revival in its own right, or whether it was rushed into print to take advantage of the popularity of Shakespeare's dramatic version.

The 'love trial' to which Lear subjects his three daughters appears both in Geoffrey of Monmouth's story, and in the old Leir play. But the desire of a father to know 'Which of you shall we say doth love us most?' is a motif found in many folk tales, for example in *Cap o'Rushes*, sometimes known as 'Love like salt'. From early childhood Shakespeare and his audiences would have been used to hearing such folk tales, which also included stories of sons who treated their fathers badly. But it is much more likely that the idea for the Gloucester plot came from another literary source that Shakespeare knew: Sir Philip

Sidney's *Arcadia* (1590). It tells the story of a Paphlagonian king who is dethroned and blinded by his illegitimate son. Shakespeare used important details from Sidney's tale, such as a storm and a duel between brothers. But in Sidney's tale the bastard son is eventually forgiven; there is no such redemption for Edmund in *King Lear*.

Two other books which fired Shakespeare's imagination contributed to the language and themes of *King Lear*: John Florio's translation of Montaigne's *Essays* (1603), and Samuel Harsnett's *A Declaration of Egregious Popish Impostures* (1603). Montaigne is thought to have influenced Shakespeare's presentation of folly and justice in *King Lear*, for example in providing the striking image of authority: 'A dog's obeyed in office' (Act 4 Scene 5, line 151). Harsnett's pamphlet, which attacks priests who conducted exorcisms as if they were theatrical spectacles, provided the demons' names that tumble from the mouth of Edgar as Poor Tom: 'Obidicut; Hobbididence Prince of dumbness; Mahu, of stealing; Modo, of murder; Flibbertigibbet, of mopping and mowing' (Quarto, Act 4 Scene 1, line 58).

What was Shakespeare's England like?

Like all writers, Shakespeare reflected in his plays the world he knew. His audiences, watching performances of *King Lear*, would recognise aspects of their own time and country. The Britain in which the pseudo-historical Lear lived was ancient and mythical. Shakespeare was not concerned with historical accuracy of setting, and *King Lear* is full of contemporary images and the customs, sights and sounds of Jacobean England. Insight into such contexts can enrich your understanding of the drama and bring you closer to the experience of a Jacobean audience.

Shakespeare may also have had in mind a recent true case of an old man cruelly treated by ungrateful daughters, but protected by a loving one, which was widely talked about at the time. Sir Brian Annesley, who had been a devoted retainer of Elizabeth I, owned considerable lands in Kent. In October 1603, Sir Brian's eldest daughter, Lady Grace Wildgoose, attempted to have her father certified as insane and unfit to manage his estate. She and her husband, Sir John Wildgoose, intended to take charge of the estate, perhaps dividing it with the second daughter, Christian. But Sir Brian's youngest daughter, significantly named Cordell, protested to the Secretary of State at the time, who gave the judgement she wanted: her father was not a lunatic and her sister's claims were denied. Some scholars have suggested that there is a play on the name Wildgoose in the Fool's line 'Winter's not gone yet, if the wild geese fly that way.' (See page 23.)

Many aspects of everyday life in Elizabethan and Jacobean England are incorporated into the play. There are references to candles and worsted stockings, peeling fruit, eel pies and toasted cheese. As Tom o'Bedlam, Edgar mentions the curfew, often signalled by a bell, which was a feature of towns and cities. Curfews were imposed at night in attempts to prevent crime or to restrict the spread of disease in times of epidemic.

'These late eclipses in the sun and moon portend no good to us', declares Gloucester (Act 1 Scene 2, lines 91–2), echoing a common superstition of the time. Unusual events in the skies were regarded as evil omens, but here Gloucester's words can be linked to real celestial phenomena: an eclipse of the moon took place on 27th September 1605, followed on 2nd October by an eclipse of the sun. The discovery and prevention of the Gunpowder plot in November of the same year (a plot to blow up the Houses of Parliament whilst the king was present) seemed proof to many that the skies could foretell disaster.

Jacobean sports and games recur in different ways throughout the play, perhaps most obviously in Lear's return from hunting just before he encounters Goneril's displeasure. When Kent trips Oswald and calls him a 'base football player', there is a subtle glance at social class assumptions of the times. Football was played by those of low social status. In contrast, tennis was for noblemen, which gives an extra significance to Lear's rebuke of Oswald (Act 1 Scene 4, line 72) for daring to 'bandy looks' with a king ('bandy' = to hit a ball to and fro). In a different key, the popular sport of bowls provides Gloucester with a metaphor for the uncompromising nature of the Duke of Cornwall:

> Whose disposition all the world well knows
> Will not be rubbed nor stopped   *(Act 2 Scene 2, lines 136–7)*

The comparison is with the bowling ball, which continues on a smooth course until it meets with a 'rub' or impediment. You can find examples of images drawn from archery and chess on pages 77–8.

There are, of course, many other examples of Shakespeare's use of contemporary practices and knowledge in the play. In addition to the topical reminders of everyday life described above there are certain significant ways in which *King Lear* reveals the condition and preoccupations of Jacobean England. What follows identifies social and cultural contexts that influenced the creation of *King Lear*: politics, social change, justice, religion, madness, death and violence.

Politics

Watching *King Lear*, Jacobean audiences would experience many resonances with their own world and recent political events. They had lived through troubled and uncertain times in the later years of Queen Elizabeth's reign. The memory of the Spanish Armada of 1588 was still fresh in their minds, and the arrival of Cordelia with the French army was likely to remind many of the attempted Spanish invasion. Although the Armada had been defeated, Elizabeth's advisers and subjects remained anxious about the problem of who would succeed her on the throne of England. Several people claimed to be her legitimate heir, but Elizabeth was stubborn and refused to be hurried into choosing a successor. In 1601, the Earl of Essex led a rebellion against her, which was quashed. However, it was not so simple for Elizabeth to quell the growing discontent of the poor.

Poverty, food shortages and unemployment were commonplace in the closing years of Elizabeth's reign and there were many riots. Bedlam beggars were familiar and deeply worrying figures who roamed the countryside pleading for charity. The myth of the golden realm of Good Queen Bess fades in the face of such social reality. Elizabeth's successor inherited a troubled land.

Elizabeth's Secretary of State, Sir Robert Cecil, worked quietly to ensure that James Stuart should take the throne of England after the queen's death. James was already king of Scotland, and had been so since infancy. When Elizabeth died in 1603, James' accession to the English throne went unopposed. He was crowned as king and the Tudor dynasty gave way to the Stuarts.

Jacobean audiences might have recognised common elements in the personalities of Lear and their own king. James, like Lear, believed passionately in his own divine right to govern and expected unquestioning obedience from all his subjects. He claimed that he had a God-given right to govern, and that it was blasphemous and unlawful to question any action taken by the king. He declared:

> The state of monarchy is the supremest thing on earth; for
> kings are not only God's lieutenants upon earth, and sit upon
> God's throne, but even by God himself they are called gods.

James also proved susceptible to the flattery of the ambitious
English courtiers who flocked to him, seeking personal advance.
Lear's belated recognition of how his own courtiers had flattered him
provided a sharp reminder to James and to his subjects that a king is
only a man like others, subject to the same human frailties: 'They told
me I was everything; 'tis a lie, I am not ague-proof.'

James' generosity towards the flattering court favourites
increasingly angered parliament. He seems to have over-estimated the
wealth of the English crown, and spent lavishly, making his way
through half a million pounds each year, an enormous sum by
contemporary standards. Shakespeare and his acting company,
originally called the Lord Chamberlain's Men, benefited directly from
his patronage. Within just a few weeks of the king's accession they
had become the King's Men, and James could call upon their services
for performances at court as he wished.

Quite what King James made of the performance of *King Lear* that
he saw on St Stephen's Night 1606 is open to speculation. The
performance would almost certainly have presented in the opening
scene the familiar rituals of deference associated with kingship,
bowing, kneeling, uncovering the head. But although the play itself
avoids direct criticism of James' profligate behaviour, it contains
allusions that held significance for contemporary audiences. When
Lear attacks Regan's elegance, some onlookers might detect a subtle
warning to a king who annually spent four times as much as Queen
Elizabeth had on fashionable clothing:

> If only to go warm were gorgeous,
> Why nature needs not what thou gorgeous wear'st,
> Which scarcely keeps thee warm   *(Act 2 Scene 4, lines 261–3)*

James had two sons, so the problem of future succession appeared
resolved. However, there was a new source of political unrest. In 1604,
James proclaimed himself king of Great Britain 'that the name of

England might be extinct'. His intention was clearly to unite England and Scotland permanently. The 'Union' debate, as it came to be known, did not receive a smooth hearing in parliament. The proposal of unification was opposed by many and, in spite of James' persistence, eventually defeated. Some scholars have argued that James specifically requested the performance of *King Lear* at court in 1606 to demonstrate that Lear's act of dividing his kingdom leads to political instability, civil war and personal tragedy. That argument is, of course, speculation, but there seems little doubt that the events of the play validate James' unionist views: partitioning a state brings dire consequences.

Social change

Another similarity between Lear and James is that both monarchs rule societies in the process of change. Both believe in hierarchical order, where each individual has a fixed place in society and understands his or her role within it. The king is securely placed at the pinnacle of that order. But throughout Shakespeare's lifetime, all kinds of challenges developed to question such assumptions.

Political thinking changed: feudal society with its strong allegiances and rigid hierarchy had virtually vanished, and discoveries in science and the New World, together with increasing wealth from commerce and manufacture, fostered new ideas about value, merit and status. Social mobility became a reality: in Elizabeth's time, gentlemen could be 'made' as well as born, and James sold knighthoods for cash. A newly prosperous gentry and commercial class challenged the power of the king and an aristocracy divided among itself. Political factions abounded, reflected in *King Lear* in the dangerous rivalry existing between Albany and Cornwall.

Newly acquired property gave power to a new kind of individual. Powerful men emerged who felt no obligation to the old feudal loyalties. They were men on the make, filled with the spirit of radical individualism, driven by self-interest. Edmund, Gloucester's unscrupulous illegitimate son, refuses to 'Stand in the plague of custom'. In rejecting tradition, he seeks to thrive by his own cunning, mocking the superstitious beliefs of his father, an upholder of the old feudal loyalty to the king. There is no place for an outdated chivalry in Edmund's moral scheme.

The corrupt Oswald is another example of the 'new man'. His self-serving character is ridiculed by the nobleman Kent ('Such smiling rogues as these'), but he is representative of an emerging class of thrusting individualists in Tudor and Jacobean England, who were motivated by self-interest, not loyalty to the old social order and its beliefs. As Michael Mangan remarks:

> . . . new mercantile capitalism tends to shatter the old order of human relationships, breaking old ties of duty and tradition, destroying communities and leading to personal excess and self-aggrandisement.

In *King Lear*, Shakespeare explores and questions that process. The acquisitiveness of Goneril, Regan and Edmund takes precedence over respect and care for their fathers. As each pursues lust or greed for power, families are divided, justice negated and the state fractured. These rampant individualists may destroy themselves, but their actions also destroy the innocent.

Justice

King Lear reflects the passionate interest of the Jacobeans in justice and the processes of law. Litigation, taking one's neighbour or some other person to court, was a common feature of life in Shakespeare's England. The play's many cross-examinations and trials would strike a familiar chord in his audiences. Lear's daughters are subjected to a 'love trial' and a 'mock trial' in their absence. Gloucester is denied the 'form of justice' of a proper trial before Cornwall and Regan. Kent and Edgar are both cross-examined, and Edmund is defeated in trial by combat. Each process leads to a judgement and a punishment, and on each occasion Shakespeare's dramatisation clearly raises questions as to whether justice has been done.

Justice is a major theme of *King Lear*, and the distinction between earthly and divine justice, human justice and justice meted out by the gods (or God) was commonly understood by Shakespeare's contemporaries. The play seems to equate earthly justice with the law of the land. Just as magistrates and judges in civil and ecclesiastical courts administered punishments, so in his madness Lear becomes absorbed by the idea that his daughters must be brought to justice. In language rich in the legal terminology of the time, he arraigns them before a bench of 'learnèd justicers' of his own choosing:

Bring in their evidence.

[*To Edgar*] Thou robèd man of justice, take thy place.

[*To the Fool*] And thou, his yoke-fellow of equity,

Bench by his side. You are o'th'commission;

Sit you too.   (Quarto, *Act 3 Scene 6*)

Later, in Act 4 Scene 5, still deranged, he imagines a 'justice' sentencing a thief, and asks, '. . . change places, and handy-dandy, which is the justice, which is the thief?' He pictures 'the great image of authority. A dog's obeyed in office.' He has learnt that there is an inherent hypocrisy in judgement itself as he imagines a beadle, another Jacobean figure of legal authority, delivering punishment. His conclusion is a damning indictment of human justice:

Thou rascal beadle, hold thy bloody hand.

Why dost thou lash that whore? Strip thy own back.

. . .

Through tattered clothes great vices do appear:

Robes and furred gowns hide all. Plate sin with gold,

And the strong lance of justice hurtless breaks;

Arm it in rags, a pygmy's straw does pierce it.

(lines 152–3; 156–9)

His denial that human justice is fair, administered with integrity and available to all, has been interpreted as a searing criticism of Jacobean society. But Lear's poor judgement has brought about his own suffering and the dissolution of his kingdom. In his role as king and judge, he now takes a more lenient stand, prepared to do what he should have done before, pardon and forgive: 'None does offend, none, I say none.'

If *King Lear* offers here a very cynical view of the possibility of earthly justice, what of divine justice? When Lear finds himself powerless against his daughters' determination he calls for divine support:

O heavens!

If you do love old men, if your sweet sway

Allow obedience, if you yourselves are old,

Make it your cause; send down and take my part.

(Act 2 Scene 4, lines 182–5)

Lear's acceptance of divine justice is grudging. The use of the conditional 'If' implies that the gods may not respond to his plea. Throughout *King Lear*, characters display various levels of belief and certainty about the efficacy of divine intervention. In Act 4 Scene 2 Albany fears that without divine intervention there can be no justice: 'Humanity must perforce prey on itself / Like monsters of the deep.' But only a few lines later, hearing of Cornwall's death, Albany claims it as proof of divine justice, 'This shows you are above, / You justicers' (lines 47–8). At the end of the play, he regards justice as having a clear scheme of returns from which

> All friends shall taste
> The wages of their virtue, and all foes
> The cup of their deservings. *(Act 5 Scene 3, lines 276–8)*

Perhaps the audience expected Albany to continue, meting out the wages and cups of deserving. But the entry of Lear, with Cordelia dead in his arms, cruelly demonstrates that there is no simple scheme of rewards or punishments, whether earthly or divine. Lear's despairing appeal emphasises the irony:

> Why should a dog, a horse, a rat have life,
> And thou no breath at all? *(lines 280–1)*

Neither human nor divine justice returns an answer to Lear's question. If the wages of virtue are indistinguishable from the 'cup of deserving' drunk by Regan, then the nature of divine justice appears as arbitrary as that of earthly justice. It seems to confirm Gloucester's bleak view of the human predicament:

> As flies to wanton boys are we to th'gods;
> They kill us for their sport. *(Act 4 Scene 1, lines 36–7)*

Religion

Shakespeare's audiences would not have believed in Gloucester's gods. Early modern England was a profoundly religious country. Whether one was Protestant or Catholic, Christianity utterly dominated most people's lives in ways difficult to identify with today. Virtually everybody cared passionately about religious matters.

Religion was ever-present, a source of both comfort and anxiety. Pervading almost every aspect of life, it is not surprising that all of Shakespeare's plays display evidence of religious influence.

The question 'Is *King Lear* a Christian play?' has been extensively explored by critics (see pages 89–90), some of whom have detected in the play a common Christian theme of a journey through pain, suffering and humiliation to love, forgiveness and wisdom. Here the issue can be briefly treated. An initial reading of *King Lear* suggests that it contains few specific references to Christianity. There are some obvious biblical echoes, such as Cordelia's 'O dear father, / It is thy business that I go about' (see page 42), and the apocalyptic nature of the storm. Most annotated editions of the play identify such references for the reader, and many productions use staging to emphasise some comparisons with Christ's passion. However, Shakespeare's sources set the story of King Lear in pre-Christian Britain, and the dramatist is especially faithful to the pagan elements of the tale.

Jacobeans would also see significance in Gloucester's attempted suicide. All Shakespeare's contemporaries worried about the state of their souls, about sin, and about what would happen after death. The question of salvation obsessed them. Would they go to heaven or hell? A son assisting his father to attempt suicide would shock many in the audience because suicide was condemned by the Church as against God's will, and suicides were believed to go straight to hell. It is possible that the shock felt by Jacobean Christians at Gloucester's suicide attempt would have been lessened by the play's setting in pagan Britain. They believed that in pre-Christian times all kinds of such 'unnatural' behaviour would have been possible.

Madness

In Shakespeare's time, people's attitudes and responses to madness were harsh and unsympathetic. The common belief was that people showing signs of madness were possessed by devils, and that they should be kept confined in a dark place and whipped. Much of Edgar's language as the madman Poor Tom is taken from a pamphlet written in 1603 which described how devils were 'cast out of lunatics' (see page 64). It was also a customary 'sport' to visit places (such as 'Bedlam') where the mentally disturbed were held, and to find entertainment in their antics.

Today, such ideas appal. Nowadays, also, doctors do not use words such as 'mad' or 'lunatic'. But Jacobean and Elizabethan audiences had a limited understanding of mental illness and no such moral scruples, and *King Lear* reflects the beliefs and language of the time.

Madness in *King Lear* is most evident in the portrayal of Lear himself, his mind tormented and unsettled by the cruel treatment he receives at the hands of his daughters. But *King Lear* does not offer simply a psychological depiction of the insanity of an individual. Human madness is reflected in disturbance at two other levels in the natural world and in society. In Act 3, Lear's inner torment is reflected in the turbulence of the storm. Lear's abdication of his powers and the division of his kingdom would have been seen as acts of political madness by Shakespeare's contemporaries. By tearing up his country, Lear kindles a storm of social frenzy that results in cruelty, blindness, madness and death.

King Lear portrays different types of mental derangement. Lear's madness is that of a selfish, autocratic old man whose will is thwarted. His moral blindness, misjudgements and lack of understanding of himself and others inevitably lead to breakdown: 'O fool, I shall go mad.' Edgar, as Poor Tom, puts on the madness of a Bedlam beggar. The Fool's 'madness' is professional, eccentric, witty, exposing weakness and folly: 'The hedge-sparrow fed the cuckoo so long, / That it's had it head bit off by it young'. Cornwall and Regan seem to become almost mad in their evil obsession with Gloucester's punishment and torture: 'Hang him instantly.' Gloucester, near to death, thinks it better to be 'distract' and lose his sorrow in 'wrong imaginations'. He views madness as a privilege, bestowing innocence upon the person lucky enough to be insane.

Death and disease

Shakespeare's contemporaries were preoccupied with death and decay in ways that are unfamiliar and even abhorrent in western society today. They looked human mortality squarely in the face. Disease and death were ever-present for most families. The average life expectancy was little more than 30 years, there was a high infant death rate, and the plague was a regular visitor to city and country alike, frequently disrupting normal life.

In his anger, Lear calls for foul air from the swamps to surround Goneril:

Infect her beauty,
You fen-sucked fogs, drawn by the powerful sun
To fall and blister.   *(Act 2 Scene 4, lines 158–60)*

Although the causes of disease were unknown, boils, plague-sores and 'embossèd carbuncles' (Act 2 Scene 4, lines 216–17) were the visible signs on the bodies of those infected with plague or other diseases. Almost every member of the audience watching the play would have seen such signs and been affected in some way by plague. Before Lear will allow blind Gloucester to kiss his hand, he says, 'Let me wipe it first; it smells of mortality' (Act 4 Scene 5, line 129), reminding Londoners of the stench of decay from carts carrying the dead through the plague-stricken streets.

Some of the harsher aspects of everyday life recur in all kinds of ways in the course of the play. With no other means of supporting themselves, the lame, the blind and the mad had to rely on charity from others, just as Edgar, in a vivid portrayal of a singularly disturbing aspect of Jacobean England, evokes the Bedlam beggars:

who with roaring voices
Strike in their numbed and mortifièd arms,
Pins, wooden pricks, nails, sprigs of rosemary;
And with this horrible object, from low farms,
Poor pelting villages, sheep-cotes, and mills,
Sometimes with lunatic bans, sometime with prayers,
Enforce their charity. 'Poor Turlygod! Poor Tom!'
                    (Act 2 Scene 3, lines 14–20)

Some of the punishments enacted in *King Lear* have their roots in Shakespeare's world, for example the use of stocks and the references to the whipping or beating of criminals and prostitutes in the streets. Other cruel sights, such as public executions and sports such as cock-fighting and bear-baiting, were the norm. However, it seems highly probable that most members of Shakespeare's audience, like today's, would flinch in horror at having to witness the naked cruelty of Gloucester's onstage blinding.

Language

The language of the play is full of variety. It shifts constantly from one register to another, sometimes formal and ceremonicus, sometimes ambiguous and enigmatic, sometimes heightened or bombastic. Even Shakespeare's contemporaries would have found some of the language difficult to understand as he used rare words or invented new ones and experimented with unfamiliar syntactical constructions. But at crucial moments the language is plain and direct, expressing the most profound feelings in the simplest words, as in the reconciliation of Lear and Cordelia in Act 4 Scene 6: 'You must not kneel', 'Do not laugh at me', 'I know you do not love me', 'No cause, no cause', 'You must bear with me.' In the play's final scene, Lear in extremity at the death of Cordelia, requests, 'Pray you, undo this button', and dies urging the appalled spectators, 'Look there, look there.'

Ben Jonson famously remarked that Shakespeare 'wanted art' (lacked technical skill). But Jonson's comment is mistaken, as is the popular image of Shakespeare as a 'natural' writer, utterly spontaneous, inspired only by his incandescent imagination. Shakespeare possessed a profound knowledge of the language techniques of his own and previous times. Behind the apparent effortlessness of the language lies a deeply practised skill. That skill is evident in *King Lear* in all kinds of ways.

What follows is a brief description of some of the language techniques Shakespeare uses in *King Lear* to intensify dramatic effect, create mood and character, and so produce memorable theatre. However, it is important always to remember that Shakespeare wrote for the stage, and that actors will therefore employ a wide range of methods, using their voices and also expressions, gestures and actions, to exploit the dramatic possibilities of the language.

The language of command

Shakespeare gives Lear an imperative style suited to a monarch utterly convinced of his right to rule and expecting his every wish to be obeyed. Lear's first words in the play are an abrupt order to Gloucester, 'Attend the lords of France and Burgundy'. Throughout the opening scenes his language bristles with the commands and imperious statements and questions of a king confident of his unshakeable authority. Even in his madness Lear strives to dictate to the elements, instructing the storm, 'Blow, winds, and crack your cheeks!' At the end of the play he is still giving orders, but the tone has changed into one of polite request, 'Pray you, undo this button. Thank you, sir.' His final words, 'Look there, look there', are an impassioned plea for confirmation that Cordelia still lives.

The language of religion

The question of whether *King Lear* is a Christian play is hotly disputed (see pages 71–2, 89–90). The setting is pagan, but the play is permeated with Christian terminology and associations; characters learn through suffering, and the language displays many of the characteristics of religious ritual:

- Prayers: 'Poor naked wretches, . . . ', 'O you mighty gods . . .'
- Oaths: 'By the sacred radiance of the sun, / The mysteries of Hecate and the night . . .'
- Sermons: 'I will preach to thee: mark . . .'
- Invocations (in which characters appeal to the heavens or the gods – Apollo, Jupiter, Juno, etc., or some other non-human agency): 'Hear, Nature, hear, dear goddess, hear', 'Thou nature art my goddess', 'Blow, winds, and crack your cheeks!', 'world world O world', 'All blest secrets . . .'
- Requests: 'hold your hand in benediction o'er me'
- Parables: in the Fool's many analogies/homilies

In her hope to find her father, and in her reconciliation with him, Cordelia's language continually affirms such Christian qualities as tolerance and understanding: 'blest', 'virtues', 'aidant', 'remediate', 'love', 'goodness', 'Cure', 'restoration', 'Repair', 'pity', 'benediction' (Act 4 Scenes 3 and 6). In the first of these scenes her words echo those of Jesus: 'O dear father, / It is thy business that I go about'.

Imagery

King Lear abounds in imagery (sometimes called 'figures' or 'figurative language'): vivid words and phrases that conjure up emotionally charged pictures in the imagination (e.g. 'How sharper than a serpent's tooth it is / To have a thankless child') and help to create the atmosphere of the play. Shakespeare seems to have thought in images, and the whole play richly demonstrates his unflagging and varied use of verbal illustration.

Early critics, such as Doctor Johnson and John Dryden, were critical of Shakespeare's fondness for imagery. They felt that many images obscured meaning and detracted attention from the subjects they represented. Over the past 200 years, however, critics, poets and audiences have increasingly valued Shakespeare's imagery. They recognise how he uses it to give pleasure, as different images stir the audience's imagination, deepen the dramatic impact of particular moments or moods, intensifying their meaning and emotional force, and provide insight into character.

Shakespeare's imagery uses metaphor, simile or personification. All are comparisons which in effect substitute one thing (the image) for another (the thing described).

- A simile compares one thing to another using 'like' or 'as': 'They flattered me like a dog'.
- A metaphor is also a comparison, suggesting that two dissimilar things are actually the same: 'Thou art a boil, / A plague-sore'.
- Personification turns all kinds of things into persons, giving them human feelings or attributes: 'Thou, Nature, art my goddess'.

Lear's words as he wakes from his torturing madness employ metaphor and simile to create a complex image that links heaven, hell and earth, Christian belief in bodily resurrection, and classical mythology (Ixion was fixed on a fiery wheel and sent spinning around the skies):

> You do me wrong to take me out o'th'grave.
> Thou art a soul in bliss, but I am bound
> Upon a wheel of fire, that mine own tears
> Do scald like molten lead.   *(Act 4 Scene 6, lines 42–5)*

Classical mythology contributes to the richness of the play's imagery, as do the everyday sports and pastimes, occupations and events of Elizabethan and Jacobean England (see pages 64–6). For example, archery supplies the imagery for a crisis in the first scene:

LEAR The bow is bent and drawn, make from the shaft.

KENT Let it fall rather, though the fork invade

    The region of my heart.   *(Act 1 Scene 1, lines 137–9)*

Kent sets himself up as the butt ('true blank' = target centre) to receive Lear's wrath, in place of Cordelia.

Kent also uses imagery from chess, sometimes called the game of kings. Threatened with execution, he claims that his own life has always been expendable in the service and protection of the king:

    My life I never held but as a pawn

    To wage against thine enemies, ne'er feared to lose it,

    Thy safety being motive.   *(lines 149–51)*

Certain image clusters recur, providing insight into crucial concerns of the play:

- Sight and blindness. Lear banishes Kent with 'Out of my sight!'. Kent's reply, 'See better, Lear', identifies Lear's moral blindness, his lack of self-knowledge. He is unable to see through the falseness of Goneril's claim to love him 'Dearer than eyesight'. Gloucester talks ironically of not needing 'spectacles' to read Edmund's traitorous letter. The villainous Edmund can clearly 'see the business'. Lear speaks of 'Old fond eyes' which threaten to shed tears. The many images of sight and blindness which pervade the play sharply underscore and emphasise the horror of the terrible, real blinding of Gloucester; Cornwall carries out Goneril's command 'Pluck out his eyes' with the brutal words 'Upon these eyes of thine I'll set my foot.' The physical pain and suffering experienced by Gloucester as a result of his blinding bring him insight into his past errors, 'I stumbled when I saw'. His new-found compassionate awareness of the nature of the world is vividly and poignantly expressed: 'I see it feelingly.'
- Animal imagery. *King Lear* resonates with images of animals. Lear likens his daughters' cruelty to that of predatory birds and beasts. He calls Goneril a 'Detested kite' whose ingratitude is 'sharper than a serpent's tooth'. Her face is 'wolvish', her tongue 'serpent-like'. In his madness he sees Goneril and Regan as 'pelican daughters', cruelly feeding on his flesh and blood. Losing his

temper, Lear calls Oswald a 'whoreson dog' and a 'cur'. As Poor Tom, Edgar 'eats the swimming frog, the toad, the tadpole, the wall-newt . . . swallows the old rat and the ditch-dog'. He describes himself as a 'hog in sloth, fox in stealth, wolf in greediness, dog in madness, lion in prey'.

Shakespeare also uses animal imagery to reflect upon what it is to be human in contrast to merely animal. Human behaviour in the play sinks to the level of the 'poor, bare, forked animal'. Gloucester's searing image reduces humans to insignificant insects, 'As flies to wanton boys are we to th'gods; / They kill us for their sport.' And perhaps Lear finally learns that it is love that defines humanity, expressed in his anguished cry over the dead body of Cordelia, 'Why should a dog, a horse, a rat have life, / And thou no breath at all?'

- Disease and pain. The political and moral disruptions which result from Lear's division of his kingdom are echoed in recurring images of pain and disease, of bodies racked and tortured. Most obviously, Lear's madness and Gloucester's blinding are parallel examples of mental and physical suffering. The language of the play is studded with images of sickness and ailments. Kent identifies Lear's banishing of Cordelia as a 'foul disease'. Lear views the Fool's criticisms as a 'pestilent gall' (an infected irritant). He curses Goneril with unhealthy vapours ('fen-sucked fogs'), hoping that they blister her. On both ungrateful daughters he wishes 'all the plagues that in the pendulous air hang'. To Lear, Goneril is 'a disease that's in my flesh', 'a boil, / A plague-sore, or embossèd carbuncle'. In his madness, Lear's ravings trigger his disgust at the thought of sexually transmitted diseases: 'There's hell, there's darkness, there is the sulphurous pit, burning, scalding, stench, consumption.'

Although disease imagery runs through the play, it is partly counterbalanced by the language of healing. Reunited with Lear in Act 4, Cordelia seeks to return him to health, and kisses him: 'restoration hang / Thy medicine on my lips'.

Antithesis

Antithesis is the opposition of words or phrases against each other, as when Lear accuses Cordelia, 'So young, and so untender?', where 'young' is set against 'untender'. This setting of word against word is one of Shakespeare's favourite language devices. He uses it extensively in all his plays. Why? Because antithesis powerfully expresses conflict through its use of opposites, and conflict is the essence of all drama.

In *King Lear*, conflict occurs in many forms: father against daughter, son against father, brother against brother, sister against sister, wife against husband. The kingdom itself is divided, and is invaded by a foreign power. Sight is set against blindness, nature against what is unnatural. Throughout, the forces of evil oppress the good.

Shakespeare's dramatic style is characterised by his concern for comparison and contrast, opposition and juxtaposition: he sets character against character, scene against scene, word against word, phrase against phrase. For example, when Gloucester is shocked by Lear's banishment of Cordelia and Kent, and angered by what he thinks is his son Edgar's perfidy, he uses antitheses to express how he sees a shattered world reflected in antagonistic family relationships:

> and the bond cracked 'twixt son and father. This villain of
> mine comes under the prediction: there's son against father.
> The king falls from bias of nature, there's father against child.
> *(Act 1 Scene 2, lines 95–8)*

Repetition

It has often been remarked that the Gloucester plot mirrors, or repeats in different form, Lear's own painful story. Similarly in the language itself, different forms of repetition run through the play, contributing to its atmosphere, creation of character and dramatic impact. In the final scene of the play, Lear's repetitions of single words convey the depth of his agony and grief for his dead daughter Cordelia:

> Howl, howl, howl, howl! *(line 231)*

> Thou'lt come no more,
> Never, never, never, never, never. *(lines 281–2)*

Similarly, the recurrence of a few key words provides a clue to some of the play's deepest preoccupations: 'nature', 'unnatural', 'love' and 'nothing'.

It is valuable to briefly trace how 'nothing' shifts its meaning as it echoes through the play. Cordelia uses it first, saying 'Nothing, my lord' to Lear's invitation to take part in his love test. She has nothing to say, no flattering words to embellish the dutiful love she feels for her father. Lear's response 'Nothing will come of nothing' adds a new meaning: if she does not declare her love for him, outdoing her sisters' professions, she will inherit nothing. The word will shift its meaning constantly in the mouth of each character no words, no wealth, no meaning, no brains, no identity.

Gloucester will reward Edmund ('it shall lose thee nothing') for his false loyalty. Kent criticises the Fool's joking advice, 'This is nothing, fool.' The Fool condemns Lear's folly, 'thou hast pared thy wit o'both sides and left nothing i'th'middle'. In further censure of Lear, the Fool gives the word yet another interpretation, loss of identity: 'I am a fool, thou art nothing'. It is a meaning which is echoed as Edgar discards his true personality, 'Edgar I nothing am'.

Goneril and Regan chillingly remind Lear that his former power will be reduced to nothing: 'What need you five and twenty? ten? or five? . . . What need one?' The consequences of Lear's rash act are devastatingly brought home to him. Many of the characters will be left with nothing at the play's end. In the most literal sense, they will be brought to nothing, losing life itself.

Shakespeare's skill in using repetition to heighten theatrical effect and deepen emotional and imaginative significance is evident in particular speeches. Repeated words, phrases, rhythms and sounds add intensity to the moment or episode. The repeated rhythms of verse are discussed below, but the play's prose also contains the same qualities of rhythmical and phrase repetition, as for example in the two long speeches by Gloucester and Edmund at Act 1 Scene 2 (lines 91–116). Repetition also occasionally occurs in rhyme, nearly always in couplets to close a scene or episode.

Lists

One of Shakespeare's favourite language methods is to accumulate words or phrases rather like a list. He had learned the technique as a schoolboy in Stratford-upon-Avon, and his skill in knowing how to use lists dramatically is evident in the many examples in *King Lear*. He intensifies a description, an atmosphere or an argument as he 'piles up' item on item, incident on incident. Some lists are brief descriptions or comprise only single words or phrases, as in Goneril's description of Lear's knights, 'Men so disordered, so deboshed and bold'. Others are more extended, perhaps most famously in Kent's angry cataloguing of Oswald's character:

> A knave, a rascal, an eater of broken meats, a base, proud,
> shallow, beggarly, three-suited, hundred-pound, filthy
> worsted-stocking knave; a lily-livered, action-taking, whoreson
> glass-gazing, superserviceable, finical rogue; one-trunk-
> inheriting slave; one that wouldst be a bawd in way of good
> service, and art nothing but the composition of a knave,
> beggar, coward, pander, and the son and heir of a mongrel
> bitch   *(Act 2 Scene 2, lines 13–19)*

The many lists in the play provide valuable opportunities for actors to vary their delivery. They usually seek to give each 'item' a distinctiveness in emphasis and emotional tone, and sometimes an accompanying action and expression.

Verse and prose

Approximately three-quarters of the play is written in verse, the remainder in prose. How did Shakespeare decide whether to write in verse or prose? One answer is that he followed theatrical convention. Prose was traditionally used by comic and low-status characters. High-status characters spoke verse. 'Comic' scenes were written in prose, as were letters and 'mad' scenes. Elizabethan and Jacobean audiences expected verse in 'serious' scenes: the poetic style was thought to be particularly suitable for moments of high drama or emotional intensity.

But Shakespeare used his judgement about which convention or principle he should follow, and in *King Lear* it is obvious that he frequently broke the 'rules'. For example, Gloucester and Edmund are both high-status characters, but in Act 1 Scene 2 their conversation is in prose. Lear is the highest-status character in the play, but in his dialogues with the Fool and his conversations with Poor Tom and the blinded Gloucester he uses prose. It may be significant that Shakespeare chose to use prose at this point, where Lear begins to realise his common humanity with those who are most wretched:

Is man no more than this? Consider him well. Thou ow'st the worm no silk, the beast no hide, the sheep no wool, the cat no perfume. Ha! Here's three on's are sophisticated; thou art the thing itself. Unaccommodated man is no more but such a poor, bare, forked animal as thou art.   *(Act 3 Scene 4, lines 92–7)*

The verse of *King Lear* displays great variation of register but is mainly in blank verse: unrhymed verse written in iambic pentameter. It is conventional to define iambic pentameter as a rhythm or metre in which each line has five stressed syllables (/) alternating with five unstressed syllables (×):

   ×   /   ×   /   ×   / ×   /   ×   /
Come not between the dragon and his wrath

At school, Shakespeare had learned the technical definition of iambic pentameter. In Greek penta means five, and iamb means a 'foot' of two syllables, the first unstressed, the second stressed (as in 'alas' = aLAS). Shakespeare practised writing in that metre, and his early plays, such as *Titus Andronicus* and *Richard III* tend to be very regular in rhythm (de-DUM de-DUM de-DUM de-DUM de-DUM), with each line 'end-stopped' (making sense on its own). But by the time he came to write *King Lear* (around 1605), Shakespeare had become very flexible and experimental in his use of iambic pentameter. The 'five-beat' metre is still present but less prominent. End-stopped lines are less frequent. There is greater use of *enjambement* (running on), where one line flows on into the next, seemingly with little or no pause. Shakespeare uses this when seeking to express the fractured emotions and dramatic intensity of a particular moment, for example:

I pant for life. Some good I mean to do,
Despite of mine own nature. Quickly send –
Be brief in it – to th'castle; for my writ
Is on the life of Lear and on Cordelia.

                                (Act 5 Scene 3, lines 217–20)

Traditional criticism

What must be remembered about critical responses to *King Lear* from the late seventeenth century until the early twentieth, is that critics did not see Shakespeare's play acted. From 1681 until well into the nineteenth century, they saw Nahum Tate's radically rewritten version (see pages 98–9). Shakespeare's own version, heavily cut, was not seen again until 1845 (in a production by Samuel Phelps), and for fifty years afterwards stage productions removed huge chunks of Shakespeare's version, perhaps most famously in Henry Irving's 1892 production which cut almost half of the lines (including much of the Gloucester plot).

Sustained critical writing on the play is generally agreed to begin with the leading eighteenth-century critic Doctor Samuel Johnson. He embodies the tradition of his time, which was to attempt to find moral instruction in the theatre. Johnson was appalled by Gloucester's blinding, and found the ending 'contrary to the natural ideas of justice'. Johnson's comment on the final scene has become perhaps the best-known early response to the play:

> I was many years ago so shocked by Cordelia's death that I know not whether I ever endured to read again the last scenes of the play until I undertook to revise them as an editor.

Other early critics followed Johnson in regretting what they saw as the play's gratuitous violence and sensationalism. But the Romantic critics of the early nineteenth century responded enthusiastically to what they read. Samuel Taylor Coleridge thought the play 'like the hurricane and the whirlpool' and called it 'the most tremendous effort of Shakespeare as a poet'. William Hazlitt judged *King Lear* 'the best of all Shakespeare's plays' because 'it is the one in which he was most in earnest'. And John Keats in his letters argued that the intensity of the poetry dispelled the 'disagreeables' portrayed. Keats' sonnet 'On sitting down to read *King Lear* once again' has become famous for its succinct descriptions of the play and the searing experience of the reader's response:

Once again, the fierce dispute
Betwixt damnation and impassioned clay
Must I burn through.

But one Romantic critic found a difficulty with *King Lear*. Charles Lamb thought the play unactable. He mocked the 'contemptible machinery' that mimics the storm, and asserted that no actor's gestures could represent Lear's suffering mind. Lamb scoffed:

> To see Lear acted, to see an old man tottering about the stage with a walking-stick, turned out of doors by his daughters in a rainy night, has nothing in it but what is painful and disgusting . . . The Lear of Shakespeare cannot be acted.

Lamb's conclusion that 'Lear is essentially impossible to be represented on a stage' was quoted with approval by Hazlitt, who thought the play 'too great for the stage'. In his view, it was a play to be read and to be best experienced in the imagination. That view was confirmed by Shelley, who judged it 'the most perfect specimen of dramatic poetry existing in the world'. Swinburne shared the same high estimation of the play on the page, but was struck by the lack of justice in the play. For him, Gloucester's remark 'As flies to wanton boys are we to th'gods; / They kill us for their sport' is the keynote of the play. His reading led him to assert:

> Requital, redemption, amends, equity, explanation, pity, mercy, are words without meaning here.

But some readers were unimpressed. The novelist Thackeray found the play 'a bore', and most notoriously Leo Tolstoy launched a withering attack on Shakespeare ('not an artist' and not even 'an average author') and *King Lear* in particular. He deplored 'the completely false "effects" of Lear running about the heath, his conversation with the Fool and all these impossible disguises, failures to recognise and the accumulating deaths'. George Orwell remarked that Tolstoy expounded the plot of *King Lear* and found it at every step to be 'stupid, verbose, unnatural, unintelligible, bombastic, vulgar, tedious and full of incredible events'. Orwell rejected Tolstoy's dismissal of the play, concluding:

The subject of Lear is renunciation, and it is only by being
wilfully blind that one can fail to understand what
Shakespeare is saying.

Nevertheless, Tolstoy's criticism is valuable because of the category
mistake it makes. Tolstoy read *King Lear* as if it were a naturalistic
novel, like his own *War and Peace* or *Anna Karenina*, rather than a
dramatic script of soaring imagination. In that misjudgement of the
genre or nature of the play are echoes of earlier criticism, such as
Doctor Johnson's concern to find moral teaching in theatre. Such
approaches are mainly concerned with character, and judge the
characters as if they were real persons. From the late eighteenth
century until well into the twentieth, that focus on moral judgement
and character has been a dominant, perhaps *the* dominant, aspect of
critical writing about *King Lear*.

The critic with whom the expression 'character study' is most
associated is A C Bradley. Around 100 years ago, Bradley delivered a
course of lectures at Oxford University which were published in 1904
as *Shakespearean Tragedy*. The book has never been out of print, and
Bradley's approach has been hugely influential.

Bradley considered only four plays as 'pure tragedies': *Hamlet*,
Othello, *King Lear* and *Macbeth*. He talked of the characters in the
tragedies as though they were real human beings existing in worlds
recognisable to modern readers. For him, each character experienced
familiar human emotions and thoughts. Bradley identified the unique
desires and motives which gave each character their particular
personality, and which evoked feelings of admiration or disapproval in
the audience. He argued that the conflict in the plays is primarily that
of an inner struggle within the characters. He saw each tragic hero
struggling with circumstances and fate, and afflicted with a fatal flaw
that causes the tragedy:

> In almost all we observe a marked one-sidedness, a
> predisposition in some particular direction; a total incapacity,
> in certain circumstances, of resisting the force which draws in
> this direction; a fatal tendency to identify the whole being with
> one interest, object, passion or habit of mind. This, it would
> seem, is, for Shakespeare, the fundamental tragic trait . . . some
> marked imperfection or defect: irresolution, precipitancy,

> pride, credulousness, excessive simplicity, excessive
> susceptibility to sexual emotions and the like . . . these
> contribute decisively to the conflict and catastrophe.

The defect of this aspect of Bradley's approach is evident. Othello does suffer from jealousy, Macbeth from ambition. But those are not their only traits. Hamlet displays a range of possible 'flaws' which contribute towards the tragedy: melancholy, hatred of Claudius, incapacity to act, over-thoughtfulness. To attribute Lear's tragedy simply to his obsession with 'filial ingratitude' would be to ignore other significant aspects of his character, not least the political misjudgement exemplified in dividing his kingdom. Like all Shakespeare's tragic heroes, Lear has more than one interest, object, passion or habit of mind'. The emphasis on character also overlooks the social context within which the tragedy occurs and which is the focus for many contemporary critics.

In his stress on the dramatic function of character, Bradley interpreted the tragedies as stories that reassured the audience or reader: tragedy was a process which, after catastrophe, paradoxically results in order, unity and goodness. Although the tragedies presented conflict and waste, evil was eventually overcome; the ending, if not happy, promised something better ahead. For Bradley, virtue and goodness triumphed in spite of suffering, adversity and death. For example, he argues that *King Lear* ends with

> a sense of law and beauty . . . a consciousness of greatness in
> pain, and of solemnity in the mystery we cannot fathom.

Modern critics are sceptical of the optimism of Bradley's thinly-veiled Christian interpretation of the play as showing 'the effect of suffering in reviving the greatness and eliciting the sweetness of Lear's nature'. They also reject Bradley's view of tragedy as mystical and indescribable ('piteous, fearful and mysterious'). In modern criticism, the origins of tragedy lie in identifiable social causes, and are capable of being resisted.

Bradley did not only focus on character in his exploration of *King Lear*. He asked crucial questions which have recurred in critical approaches ever since, for example: Is it a good stage play? Is it well constructed? Is the opening scene credible? Is the death of Cordelia dramatically justifiable? Was Lear redeemed? Is the play fundamentally pessimistic? Does it reflect Shakespeare's personal feelings?

Although Bradley has fallen from critical favour, his influence is still evident, and as pages 118–24 show, it is difficult to avoid talking or writing about characters as if they were living people and making moral judgements on them. Furthermore, Bradley's criticism extended more widely than character alone and has provided a starting point for different approaches to the play which developed throughout the twentieth century.

Caroline Spurgeon greatly extended Bradley's examination of the play's imagery. In her book *Shakespeare's Imagery and What it Tells Us*, Spurgeon identifies patterns of imagery in each of Shakespeare's plays. She finds in *King Lear* 'only one overpowering and dominating continuous image', that of a body racked and tortured. She notes that the animal imagery distinctly augments the sensation of horror and bodily pain, and she gives many examples of how the play persistently provides metaphorical reminders of a human body in anguished movement:

> Tugged, wrenched, beaten, pierced, stung, scourged,
> dislocated, flayed, gashed, scalded, tortured and finally broken
> on the rack.

Today, Spurgeon's pioneering work is much criticised, not only for its narrow focus (she avoids any mention of sexual imagery, for example), but also for its bardolatry (uncritical praise of all Shakespeare's writing) and its endeavour to identify in the imagery Shakespeare's own likes, dislikes and personality. Notwithstanding such flaws, her work is immensely valuable in encouraging the study of imagery, which is such a distinctive feature of every Shakespeare play. Later critics have stressed the importance of other image clusters in the play: sight and blindness, clothes, madness in reason and reason in madness, the gods, nature. You can find more on imagery in the Language section (see pages 76–9).

Such image clusters usually lead into discussion of how they express or embody the themes of the play. For example, John F Danby uses the concept of 'nature' to interpret the play, seeing it as expressing the conflict between two views of nature, one benign, rational and divinely ordered, the other governed by self-interest and appetite. Many other critics have pointed out how frequently 'Nature', 'natural', or 'unnatural', appear in the play, expressing many different meanings, often resonating with irony: a child's birthright, illegitimate, the bonds of love and loyalty, the natural world, a goddess, the given order or hierarchy of things or society, obligations and duties, universal laws, established authority and human nature itself (benign and forgiving or malign and selfish).

An alternative example of a thematic approach is expressed by Frank Kermode:

> In this play, not for the first time, Shakespeare concerns
> himself with the contrast between the two bodies of the king;
> one lives by ceremony, administers justice in a furred gown,
> distinguished by regalia which set him above nature. The other
> is born naked, subject to disease and pain, and protected only
> by the artifices of ceremony from natural suffering and
> nakedness. So Lear is stripped, and moves from the
> ceremonies of the first scene to the company of a naked
> 'natural', the thing itself. The play deals with what intervenes
> between our natural and our artificially comfortable
> conditions: ceremony, justice, love, evil.

In a different approach, G Wilson Knight's influential *The Wheel of Fire* identifies 'the comedy of the grotesque' that Knight finds in the play. He argues that it displays realities that are in turn 'absurd, hideous, pitiful' as it moves from the absurdity of the opening scene through the 'fantastic incongruity' of parent and child opposed, the Fool's perception of humour in heart-wrenching situations, Edgar's 'fantastic impersonation' and the ludicrousness of Gloucester's suicide attempt. He notes the 'demonic laughter that echoes in the Lear universe', and sees the play as crucially about 'a tremendous soul . . . incongruously geared to a puerile intellect'. Nevertheless, Knight possesses the same view of the play as Bradley, seeing in it the Christian notion of redemption: Cordelia embodies the principle of ideal love, and Lear is redeemed (like Job in the Bible) through suffering. But in a judgement that prefigures that of Jan Kott (see page 93), Knight claims about *King Lear*:

In no tragedy of Shakespeare do incident and dialogue so
recklessly and miraculously walk the tight-rope of our pity
over the depths of bathos and absurdity.

Wilson Knight is one of many critics who have detected Christian
patterns and values embedded in the play, in particular the Christian
doctrines of redemption and patience, heaven and hell. Such critics
have sought to find religious meaning in the suffering, even picturing
Lear as Christ-like. For example, J C Maxwell described *King Lear* as 'a
Christian play about a pagan world'. L C Knights thought of it as
'directed towards affirmation in spite of everything'.

Other critics have challenged such views. Clifford Leech argued
that a Christian tragedy is impossible; Nicholas Brooke found the
ending 'without any support from systems of moral or artistic belief at
all'; R G Hunter found the play 'harshly pagan' and argued that in it
Shakespeare dramatised the possibility that there is no God; and John
Holloway perceived Lear as a scapegoat, and claimed that the ending
provided meagre consolation. Probably the two best-known critics of
the Christian interpretation of *King Lear* are Barbara Everett and W R
Elton. Everett criticised interpretations that attempted to turn the
tragedy into an allegory or miracle or morality play. She argues that
the play is the product of a Christian world-view, but lacks doctrinal
and allegorical Christian dimensions. She points out that the scenes
which are most full of explicitly 'Christian' phrasing, or suggestion, or
feeling, are confined, on the whole, to the period between the storm
scenes and the entry of Lear with Cordelia dead in his arms. She
argues that the mood and tone of these scenes may be caused 'as much
by artistic reasons as by moral design'. Everett concludes:

It is obviously impossible to decide, simply, whether or not
King Lear is a 'Christian' play.

William R Elton in *King Lear and the Gods* argues that Lear is not
regenerated, that providence is not operative, and that the last act
shatters 'the foundations of faith itself'. He concludes that the play is
not 'a drama of meaningful suffering and redemption, within a just
universe ruled by providential higher powers' and that its ironical
structure is calculated to destroy faith in both poetic justice and divine
justice.

Modern criticism

Throughout the second half of the twentieth century and in the twenty-first, critical approaches to Shakespeare have radically challenged the style and assumptions of the traditional approaches described above. New critical approaches argue that traditional interpretations, with their heavy emphasis on character or metaphysical abstractions ('evil', 'justice', etc.), are individualistic and misleading. The traditional focus on personalities and emotions ignores society and history, and so divorces literary, dramatic and aesthetic matters from their social context. Furthermore, their detachment from the real world makes them elitist, sexist and unpolitical.

Modern critical perspectives therefore shift the focus to how social conditions (of the world of the play and of Shakespeare's England) are reflected in characters' relationships, language and behaviour. Modern criticism also concerns itself with how changing social assumptions at different periods of time have affected interpretations of the play. This section will explore how recent critical approaches to Shakespeare can or have been used to address *King Lear*. Like traditional criticism, contemporary perspectives include many different approaches but share common features Modern criticism:

- is sceptical of 'character' approaches (but often uses them);
- concentrates on political, social and economic factors (arguing that these factors determined Shakespeare's creativity and affect audiences' and critics' interpretations);
- identifies contradictions, fragmentation and disunity in the plays;
- questions the possibility of 'happy' or 'hopeful' endings, preferring ambiguous, unsettling or sombre endings;
- produces readings that are subversive of existing social structures;
- identifies how the plays express the interests of dominant groups, particularly rich and powerful males;
- insists that 'theory' (psychological, social, etc.) is essential to produce valid readings;
- often expresses its commitment to a particular cause or perspective (for example, to feminism, or equality, or political change);
- argues all readings are political or ideological readings (and that traditional criticism falsely claims to be objective);
- argues that traditional approaches have always interpreted

Shakespeare conservatively, in ways that confirm and maintain the interests of the elite or dominant class.

The following discussion is organised under headings which represent major contemporary critical perspectives (political, feminist, performance, psychoanalytic, postmodern). But it is vital to appreciate that there is often overlap between the categories, and that to pigeonhole any example of criticism too precisely is to reduce its value.

Political criticism

'Political criticism' is a convenient label for approaches concerned with power and social structure in the world of the play, in Shakespeare's time and in our own. It exposes the economic and social roots of injustice and inequality. In such approaches a central assumption is that in tragedy individuals are destroyed by the workings of political power and historical forces, not by some 'tragic flaw' or by chance or fate or the gods. Tragedy is seen as caused by human beings, it is not divinely ordained. Here, *King Lear* is often viewed as portraying the conflict between a rigidly hierarchical feudal world of shared values and an emerging new society of thrusting individuals who reject old loyalties and beliefs.

In this interpretation, Lear's England reflects Shakespeare's changing world, and Edmund is the model of the 'new man' governed by self-interest: he knows that disasters and bastardy are not caused by the stars, but are the result of human action and belief. Lear fails to realise the consequences of giving away power. Justice is in the hands of the powerful, and only in his suffering does Lear feel pity for 'Poor naked wretches' and see clearly that 'A dog's obeyed in office'. Similarly, only in his torment does Gloucester perceive that social justice requires removal of gross inequality:

> So distribution should undo excess,
> And each man have enough.   *(Act 4 Scene 1, lines 65–6)*

Kiernan Ryan, writing in 1993, claimed that 'a new era' in the study of *King Lear* had begun 'over the past ten years', and that the reasons for the shift in direction of criticism 'can be summed up in one word: politics'. But as you will find below, the single word 'politics' does not sufficiently express the variety of modern criticism, and 'political' approaches to *King Lear* began well before Ryan's estimated date. For example in 1971, J W Lever in *The Tragedy of State* had firmly rejected the focus on the tragic hero in favour of concentration on the society in which he exists, arguing that tragedy 'is not primarily treatments of characters with a so-called "fatal flaw", whose downfall is brought about by the decree of just if inscrutable powers . . . the fundamental flaw is in the world they inhabit: in the political state, the social order it upholds'. Even earlier, in 1964, the Marxist critic Arnold Kettle had identified the 'heartless rationalisation' of the 'new people' who bring down Lear, and had argued that the play was an indictment of the social conditions of Shakespeare's times. One year later, a well-known challenge to traditional approaches was made by the Polish critic Jan Kott.

Kott fought with the Polish army and underground movement against the Nazis in the Second World War (1939–45), and had direct experience of the suffering and terror caused by Stalinist repression in Poland in the years after the war. Kott's book *Shakespeare our Contemporary* (1965) saw parallels between the violence and cruelty of the modern world and the worlds of tyranny and despair that Shakespeare depicted in his tragedies. The importance of the title of Kott's book cannot be overstressed. It emphasises that Shakespeare is modern in his bleak view of human history and humanity itself.

Kott argues that history, rather than fate or the gods, is the cause of tragedy. He uses the image of 'the Grand Mechanism' of history: a great staircase up which characters tread to their doom, each step 'marked by murder, perfidy, treachery'. It does not matter if a character is good or bad, history will overwhelm them. Characters have little or no power over their lives, but are swept aside by inevitable social and historical forces beyond their control.

In this grim scenario of history, Kott equates *King Lear* with Samuel Beckett's *Endgame*: a play whose grotesque ending produces no catharsis (purging of the emotions). He identifies the absurdity of the fall from Dover cliff and, interpreting the blinded Gloucester as Everyman wandering through the world, claims that the theme of *King Lear* is 'an enquiry into the meaning of this journey, into the existence or non-existence of heaven and hell' and 'the decay and fall of the world'. For Kott, the play shows that:

> All bonds, all laws, whether divine, natural or human, are
> broken . . . Social order, from the kingdom to the family, will
> crumble into dust . . . There are only huge Renaissance
> monsters devouring one another like beasts of prey.

Before Kott's book was published in English, he discussed his
interpretation with the director Peter Brook, and their discussion
strongly influenced Brook's notoriously bleak production in 1962 (see
page 100). Many later productions have also been affected by Kott's
view of how the play's tragic grotesquerie is appropriate to the modern
world. Kott's interpretations have been much criticised, but they can
be seen as forerunners of new approaches which focus on the social
and political contexts and causes of tragedy. Kiernan Ryan's
interpretation is notable in arguing that *King Lear*, like Shakespeare's
other tragedies, does not just question the inequalities and injustices
of Shakespeare's England, but offers the liberating vision that human
suffering is not inevitable (as in traditional views of tragedy):

> *Lear* dramatises the cost in potential equality and mutual
> fulfilment of the humanly contrived structures of division and
> domination responsible for the tragedy.

Jonathan Dollimore's key book, *Radical Tragedy* (1989), similarly
argues that criticism should centre instead upon society, particularly
on 'class, sexuality, imperialist and colonial exploitation'. Dollimore
has no doubt about the relationships between *King Lear* (and other
Jacobean tragedies) and the state. He claims that in those plays,
Shakespeare and other playwrights actively question and subvert
contemporary political power and ideology, making visible the power
struggles within Jacobean society. For Dollimore, the tragedies expose
the injustices and inequalities of that society. They question the beliefs
and structures which maintain those unfair practices, for example
monarchical rule in which Queen Elizabeth or King James and a small
number of aristocrats enjoyed total power and huge privilege.

Dollimore's attack on character study is equally fundamental. He
challenges the 'central assumptions of the traditional reading of
character, human nature and individual identity' of earlier criticism.
For Dollimore, human personality is determined by, and reflects, the
historical conditions of the time. It is not stable or unified, but

fractured and full of contradictions. He argues that the malcontents in the tragedies, like Edmund in *King Lear*, are representations of such unstable, fractured personalities, and are both the victims and agents of social corruption. As such, they reveal the true nature of society:

> the Jacobean malcontent . . . is not the antithesis of social process but its focus . . . the focus of political, social, and ideological contradiction.

Many 'political' critics avoid speculating about Shakespeare's own politics or his intentions in writing his tragedies. But one Marxist critic, Victor Kiernan, attempts to root the tragedies squarely in Shakespeare's own experience of life in Elizabethan and Jacobean England. Kiernan argues that Shakespeare's concern was for the poor whose toil and suffering paid for the pleasures and follies of the rich, and that he was haunted by the image of the poor man in the stocks. Kiernan thinks that Shakespeare's tragic vision

> must have started from something personal, some dislocation of his own life . . . which opened his eyes wider to the world round him and to its martyrdom.

Kiernan's assumption results in social interpretations. In the harsh world of *King Lear*, Kiernan sees a reflection of the ruthlessness of the Jacobean age. An older, more stable age has passed, and now 'men are as the time is', pitiless and self-seeking. He argues that although the play shows very little of the hungry poor, and nothing of riotous crowds,

> Shakespeare works on our imagination instead, keeping the poor an invisible but compelling presence . . . Shakespeare leaves us to hope that some day the masses will stand up for themselves.

Feminist criticism

Feminist criticism is the fastest growing and most widespread of all modern approaches to tragedy. It is part of the wider project of feminism, which aims to achieve rights and equality for women in social, political and economic life. It challenges sexism: those beliefs and practices that result in the oppression and subordination of women. Feminism reveals how gender roles are shaped to the disadvantage of women in family, work, politics and religion. It exposes the male prejudice that for millennia has portrayed women as different from and inferior to men. For example, in Shakespeare's time the pernicious views of John Knox, a Scottish Protestant preacher, expressed in his *First Blast of the Trumpet against the Monstrous Regiment of Women* (1558), were enthusiastically believed. Knox claimed that nature creates women as

> weak, frail, impatient, feeble and foolish: and experience hath declared them to be unconstant, variable, cruel, and lacking the spirit of counsel and regiment ('regiment' = order, self-control).

Feminist criticism opposes the maleness of traditional criticism which was written by men and which often stereotypes or distorts the woman's point of view. This 'male ownership' of criticism meant that it was men who determined what questions were to be asked of a play, and which answers were acceptable. In contrast, feminists examine how female experience is portrayed in criticism of tragedy, and expose how women's feelings and actions are neglected, repressed or misrepresented.

Feminist criticism, like any 'approach', takes a wide variety of forms. Nonetheless it is possible to identify certain major concepts or concerns which recur in feminist critical writing on *King Lear*:

- Patriarchy (male domination of women). For much of the play, Lear treats his daughters as subordinates who must obey his every whim. Like many other Shakespearean fathers, Lear is enraged when his daughters disobey him. Patriarchy is interpreted as the cause of the tragedy. At the end of the play all three daughters are dead, and women have no part in the new order which is uncompromisingly male.
- Misogyny (male hatred of women). Male language frequently demeans women as for example when Lear threatens and curses his daughters.
- Sexual disgust. Lear raves that the female genitals are the source of evil: 'But to the girdle do the gods inherit; / Beneath is all the

fiend's. / There's hell, there's darkness, there is the sulphurous pit' (Act 4 Scene 5, lines 122–4). Women are the source of lust, and Goneril and Regan are destroyed by their desire for Edmund.

- Unnaturalness. His daughters' defiance and resistance is seen by Lear as reversing the natural order of things (which he sees as female subordination and compliance to male wishes). He curses his daughters as 'unnatural hags'.
- Women as property. Lear regards Cordelia as a possession, to be disposed of as he sees fit.
- Positive views of women. Feminist interpretations of Goneril (and, to a lesser extent, Regan) find justification in their resistance to their father's selfish and oppressive behaviour. The feminist concept of 'sisterhoods of resistance' is sometimes used to describe how Goneril and Regan combine to defy Lear's authority.
- Stereotyping. Feminist critics challenge the traditional portrayal of women as examples of 'virtue' or 'vice'. In arguing for equality, feminists demonstrate that Goneril and Regan are, like the male characters, complex and flawed, experiencing similar emotions to men and suffering like them.

Feminist approaches to tragedy vary widely because there is of course more than one 'woman's point of view'. One feminist critic, Jacqueline Dusinberre, in *Shakespeare and the Nature of Women* (1975), claims that 'drama from 1590 to 1625 is feminist in sympathy'. She argues strongly that Shakespeare 'saw men and women as equal in a world which declared them as unequal'. Her views are echoed by others who argue that *King Lear* invites dissent from misogyny and patriarchy, and can be interpreted and performed in ways that expose patriarchy as vicious and unjust.

But other feminist critics do not share Dusinberre's view. They seek to expose the misogyny and patriarchy that degrades women. For example Kathleen McLuskie argues that *King Lear* presents a conventional and conservative male view of the world, seeing it as a patriarchal morality play in which the female characters are either sanctified (Cordelia) or demonised (Goneril and Regan). She sees a 'mystification of the real socio-sexual relations' in the play, so that audience sympathy is manipulated to evoke compassion for Lear, despite the loathing he displays towards women. She concludes:

The misogyny of *King Lear*, both the play and its hero, is constructed out of an ascetic tradition which presents women as the source of the primal sin of lust, combining with concerns about the threat to the family posed by female insubordination.

Such readings (like all critical interpretations) raise the question of whether they are what Shakespeare intended. Was he purposefully challenging female stereotyping? Whilst many critics today argue that Shakespeare's intentions can never be known, a distinctive feature of feminist criticism is to suggest that *King Lear* subjects patriarchal conventions to critical scrutiny, exposing them as irrational and repressive.

Performance criticism

Performance criticism fully acknowledges that *King Lear* is a play: a script to be performed by actors before an audience. It examines all aspects of the play in performance: its staging in the theatre or on film and video. Performance criticism focuses on Shakespeare's stagecraft and the semiotics of theatre (words, costumes, gestures, etc.), together with the 'afterlife' of the play (what happened to *King Lear* after Shakespeare wrote it). That involves scrutiny of how productions at different periods have presented the play. As such, performance criticism appraises how the text has been cut, added to, rewritten and rearranged to present a version felt appropriate to the times.

The first recorded performance of the play was for King James I at the palace of Whitehall, London, on St Stephen's Night (26th December), 1606. The play had almost certainly also been performed a number of times that year at the Globe Theatre on London's Bankside. The king may have requested a performance of this particular play because it portrayed the folly of dividing a kingdom (see pages 67–8) or perhaps it was chosen because its subject matter and themes were appropriate for the festival. The feast of St Stephen was celebrated by offering hospitality to the poor, and the set Bible readings for the day emphasised the need to be patient even in times of suffering.

The play does not seem to have been popular. Only three other performances are known to have taken place up to 1681. In that year, Nahum Tate published his own radically revised adaptation, which was the only version staged until well into the nineteenth century.

Tate's dedication to his rewriting of *King Lear* records that he found Shakespeare's play

> a heap of jewels, unstrung and unpolished; yet so dazzling in their disorder, that I soon perceived I had seized a treasure . . . the method necessarily threw me on making the tale conclude in a success of the innocent distressed persons: otherwise I must have encumbered the stage with dead bodies.

Tate's response to that 'heap of jewels' was to ensure that good triumphed unequivocally over evil. He ensured that the play really did end 'in a success of the innocent distressed persons': Lear survives and is restored to his throne, Gloucester lives, Cordelia and Edgar are virtuous lovers, the King of France disappears, as does the Fool (humour being judged not suitable to tragedy). Around 800 of Shakespeare's lines are cut. For 150 years audiences saw only Tate's version, and the major actors of the times such as David Garrick and Kemble were acclaimed for their performances as Lear.

In 1823 Edmund Kean restored the tragic ending, and in 1838 William Charles Macready brought back the Fool (played by a woman). But the play continued to be heavily cut, and Victorian productions followed the fashion of the times for 'historical authenticity', which in practice resulted in spectacular sets suggesting ancient Britain, Stonehenge, or even Roman temples. A mish-mash of costumes sometimes conveyed the impression of Anglo-Saxon England.

The twentieth century saw a return to much simpler stagings of the play. Although the tradition of extravagant productions lingered on, most productions no longer attempted to create an impression of realism. The influential critic and director Harley Granville Barker comprehensively rebutted the pessimism of Lamb (see page 85) and Bradley, who doubted the play could be effectively staged. Granville Barker's *Prefaces to Shakespeare: King Lear* gives detailed practical guidance based on his starting assumption about the play that

> Shakespeare meant it to be acted, and he was a very practical playwright.

Granville Barker shows how the storm scene can make superbly compelling theatre, and how the Gloucester plot is a fully developed parallel to the main plot. Under his influence, Shakespeare's full text (usually a conflation of the Folio and the Quarto) was played with few cuts. Stages were cleared of the clutter of historical detail and illusionist sets and properties, and productions aimed to recapture the non-illusory conditions of the Elizabethan bare stage. That implied a minimum of scenery, scenes flowing swiftly into each other, and a concern for clear speaking of Shakespeare's language.

King Lear has become one of Shakespeare's most frequently performed plays. Since 1945 there have been many more performances than in all the preceding 350 years. Space makes it impossible to detail the great variety of ways in which *King Lear* has been performed throughout the twentieth and into the twenty-first century. Lear himself has been played in any number of different ways: as an out-and-out tyrant, as a genial father, as coldly demanding from the start or as warmly affectionate.

Peter Brook's 1962 Royal Shakespeare production was directly influenced by Jan Kott's bleak and absurdist view of the contemporary world (see pages 93–4). There was no hope of redemption or affirmation in Brook's vision. Nihilism and cruelty dominated: the servants who kindly help the blinded Gloucester were cut, as was Edmund's repentance and attempt to avert the murder of Cordelia. Paul Scofield's austere Lear seemed designed to resist audience sympathy. In the hostile universe Brook created, nature and the gods were clearly indifferent to human suffering. The audience's final view of the play was of Edgar dragging away the corpse of his brother.

Antony Sher's dazzling performance as a red-nosed Fool for the Royal Shakespeare Company in 1982 received great acclaim, but some critics felt that his rapport with the audience diminished Edmund's role as the character who traditionally establishes a direct link with the audience.

Psychoanalytic criticism

In the twentieth century, psychoanalysis became a major influence on the understanding and interpretation of human behaviour. The founder of psychoanalysis, Sigmund Freud, explained personality as the result of unconscious and irrational desires, repressed memories or wishes, sexuality, fantasy, anxiety and conflict. Freud's theories have had a strong influence on criticism and stagings of

Shakespeare's plays, most obviously on *Hamlet* in the well-known claim that Hamlet suffers from an Oedipus complex.

Psychoanalytic interpretations can often be seen in performance, when an actor's behaviour or style of speech hints at what lies behind a character's words. For example Judi Dench, playing Regan, stuttered as she spoke to Lear. Her explanation reached back into what she saw as Regan's early experience, interpreting her 'filial ingratitude' as a reaction against the parental tyranny she had endured. An actor's search for motivation, for discovering how a character comes to be as he or she is, frequently results in a form of psychoanalytic investigation (as indeed does much character criticism).

King Lear dramatises some of the deepest preoccupations of the human subconscious. Its searing portrayal of Lear's irrationality, of fractured family relationships, and of different kinds of mental disturbance clearly holds strong appeal to psychoanalytically inclined critics. Norman Holland in *Psychoanalysis and Shakespeare* reports that Freud himself 'approached Lear as a child choosing the ultimate mother, mute Death', and notes that *King Lear* 'has evoked an intricate variety of psychoanalytic readings'. They include

- Lear as old man and father. He has been variously seen as an old man harbouring incestuous desires for his daughters, a father who 'eliminates his wife and marries his daughters', a sadist whose impulses make him a victim of circumstance, a neurotic who cannot tolerate delaying his gratifications, a schizophrenic and sexual fantasist.
- Lear as child. Here, interpretations have claimed he is a child acting out his realisation that he is not omnipotent, a child troubled and confused by his parents' secret sexual life together (for example in his rage at being locked out), a 'child's orphan' (here Cordelia is seen as Lear's mother, nourishing him), a narcissist who wishes to become a child again and bathe in limitless love.
- Interpretations as myth, ritual or folklore. The Cinderella-like quality of the play is often remarked: 'Once upon a time there was an old king with three daughters. The older two were harsh, but the youngest . . .'.
- Lear as sacrificial victim. Lear's suffering is to redeem society's ills, and Regan becomes a 'castrator'.

- Sibling rivalry. Lear's daughters and Gloucester's sons represent two aspects of the child: loving versus hostile, loyal versus cruel.

Some critics combine approaches. For example Coppelia Kahn's interpretation is an example of feminist psychoanalytic theory. In her significantly titled essay 'The absent mother in *King Lear*', Kahn's endeavour is 'like an archaeologist, to uncover the hidden mother in the hero's inner world'. As such she claims that the tragedy shows 'the failure of a father's power to command love in a patriarchal world and the emotional price he pays for wielding power'. Lear realises at the end that Cordelia is the 'only loving woman in his world, the one person who could possibly fulfil the needs he has, in such anguish, finally come to admit'. She interprets the play as a 'tragedy of masculinity', and argues that in Lear's patriarchal world 'masculine identity depends on repressing the vulnerability, dependency and capacity for feeling which are called "feminine"'.

The interpretations listed above reveal the obvious weaknesses in applying psychoanalytic theories to *King Lear*. They cannot be proved or disproved, they neglect historical, political and social factors that are fundamental to the play, and they are often highly speculative. Psychoanalytic approaches are therefore frequently accused of imposing interpretations based on theory rather than upon Shakespeare's text. Nevertheless, the play's evident concern with disjunctions in family relationships offers rich opportunities for psychoanalytic interpretations.

Postmodern criticism

Postmodern criticism (sometimes called 'deconstruction') is not always easy to understand because it is not centrally concerned with consistency or reasoned argument. It does not accept that one section of the story is necessarily connected to what follows, or that characters relate to each other in meaningful ways. Because of such assumptions, postmodern criticism is sometimes described as 'reading against the grain' or less politely as 'textual harassment'. The approach therefore has obvious drawbacks in providing a model for examination students who are expected to display reasoned, coherent argument, and respect for the evidence of the text.

Postmodernism often revels in the cleverness of its own use of language, and accepts all kinds of anomalies and contradictions in a spirit of playfulness or 'carnival'. It abandons any notion of the organic unity of the play, and rejects the assumption that a Shakespeare play possesses clear patterns or themes. Some postmodern critics even deny the possibility of finding meaning in language. They claim that words simply refer to other words, and so any interpretation is endlessly delayed (or 'deferred', as the deconstructionists say). Others focus on minor or marginal characters, or on loose ends, gaps and uncertainties (which they call 'aporia') or silences in the play, claiming that these features, often overlooked as unimportant, reveal significant truths about the play.

Postmodern approaches to *King Lear* are most clearly seen in stage productions which employ 'a mixture of styles'. The label 'postmodern' is applied to productions which self-consciously show little regard for consistency in character, or for coherence in telling the story. Characters are dressed in costumes from very different historical periods, and carry both modern and ancient weapons. Ironically, Shakespeare himself has been regarded as a postmodern writer in the way he mixes genres in his plays, for example comedy with tragedy in *King Lear*.

Kiernan Ryan's *New Casebook* (see page 127) provides examples of such approaches by Felperin, Eagleton and Goldberg. All make demands on the reader, and all are concerned with what they variously describe as the enigma, mutual negations and impossibilities of the play. For theorists who hold such assumptions, the play's frequent repetition of 'nothing' has obvious appeal. Goldberg's comment displays the reductionism and pessimism about the possibility of meaning that so often characterises postmodern criticism:

> In *King Lear*, nothing comes of nothing, and the very language which would seem (to us) solidly to locate the world slides into an abyss, an uncreating, annihilative nothingness.

Organising your responses

The purpose of this section is to help you improve your writing about *King Lear*. It offers practical guidance on two kinds of tasks: writing about an extract from the play and writing an essay. Whether you are answering an examination question, preparing coursework (term papers) or carrying out research into your own chosen topic, this section will help you organise and present your responses.

In all your writing, there are three vital things to remember:

- *King Lear* is a play. Although it is usually referred to as a 'text', *King Lear* is not a book, but a script intended to be acted on a stage. So your writing should demonstrate an awareness of the play in performance as theatre.
- *King Lear* is not a presentation of 'reality'. It is a dramatic construct in which the playwright, through theatre, engages the emotions and intellect of the audience. Through discussion of his handling of language, character and plot, your writing should reveal how Shakespeare uses themes and ideas, attitudes and values, to give insight into crucial social, moral and political dilemmas of his time – and yours.
- How Shakespeare learned his craft. As a schoolboy, and in his early years as a dramatist, Shakespeare used all kinds of models or frameworks to guide his writing. But he quickly learned how to vary and adapt the models to his own dramatic purposes. This section offers frameworks that you can use to structure your writing. As you use them, follow Shakespeare's example! Adapt them to suit your own writing style and needs.

Writing about an extract

It is an expected part of all Shakespeare study that you should be able to write well about an extract (sometimes called a 'passage') from the play. An extract is usually between 30 and 70 lines long, and you are invited to comment on it. The instructions vary. Sometimes the task is very briefly expressed:

- Write a detailed commentary on the following passage.

- Write about the effect of the extract on your own thoughts and feelings.

At other times, a particular focus is specified for your writing:

- With close reference to the language and imagery of the passage, show in what ways it helps to establish important issues in the play.
- Analyse the style and structure of the extract, showing what it contributes to your appreciation of the play's major concerns.

In writing your response, you must of course take account of the precise wording of the task and ensure that you concentrate on each particular point specified. But however the invitation to write about an extract is expressed, it requires you to comment in detail on the language. You should identify and evaluate how the language reveals character, contributes to plot development, offers opportunities for dramatic effect and embodies crucial concerns of the play as a whole. These 'crucial concerns' are also referred to as 'themes', or 'issues', or 'preoccupations' of the play.

The following framework is a guide to how you can write a detailed commentary on an extract. Writing a paragraph on each item will help you bring out the meaning and significance of the extract and show how Shakespeare achieves his effects.

Paragraph 1: Locate the extract in the play and say who is on stage.
Paragraph 2: State what the extract is about and identify its structure.
Paragraph 3: Identify the mood or atmosphere of the extract.
Paragraphs 4–8:
    Diction (vocabulary)
    Imagery
    Antithesis
    Repetition
    Lists

These paragraphs analyse how Shakespeare achieves his effects. They concentrate on the language of the extract, showing the dramatic effect of each item, and how the language expresses crucial concerns of the play.

Paragraph 9: Staging opportunities
Paragraph 10: Conclusion

Although the framework identifies ten paragraphs, you may of course choose to write more than one paragraph under any heading.

The following example uses the framework to show how the paragraphs making up the essay might be written. The framework headings (in bold), would not of course appear in your essay. They are presented only to help you see how the framework is used.

Extract

Enter CORNWALL, REGAN, GLOUCESTER, *[and] Servants*

LEAR Good morrow to you both.
CORNWALL   Hail to your grace.
                    Kent here set at liberty
REGAN I am glad to see your highness.
LEAR Regan, I think you are. I know what reason
      I have to think so. If thou shouldst not be glad,
      I would divorce me from thy mother's tomb,   5
      Sepulch'ring an adultress. [*To Kent*] O are you free?
      Some other time for that. Belovèd Regan,
      Thy sister's naught. Oh Regan, she hath tied
      Sharp-toothed unkindness, like a vulture here –
      I can scarce speak to thee – thou'lt not believe   10
      With how depraved a quality – oh Regan!
REGAN I pray you, sir, take patience. I have hope
      You less know how to value her desert
      Than she to scant her duty.
LEAR   Say? How is that?
REGAN I cannot think my sister in the least   15
      Would fail her obligation. If, sir, perchance
      She have restrained the riots of your followers,
      'Tis on such ground and to such wholesome end
      As clears her from all blame.
LEAR   My curses on her.
REGAN O sir, you are old,   20
      Nature in you stands on the very verge
      Of his confine. You should be ruled and led
      By some discretion that discerns your state
      Better than you yourself. Therefore I pray you
      That to our sister you do make return;   25
      Say you have wronged her.
LEAR   Ask her forgiveness?

Do you but mark how this becomes the house?
[*Kneels*] 'Dear daughter, I confess that I am old;
Age is unnecessary; on my knees I beg
That you'll vouchsafe me raiment, bed, and food.'   30
REGAN Good sir, no more: these are unsightly tricks.
    Return you to my sister.
LEAR [*Rising*]   Never, Regan.
    She hath abated me of half my train,
    Looked black upon me, struck me with her tongue
    Most serpent-like upon the very heart.   35
    All the stored vengeances of heaven fall
    On her ingrateful top! Strike her young bones,
    You taking airs, with lameness.
CORNWALL   Fie, sir, fie.
LEAR You nimble lightnings, dart your blinding flames
    Into her scornful eyes! Infect her beauty.   40
    You fen-sucked fogs, drawn by the powerful sun
    To fall and blister.
REGAN O the blessed gods! So will you wish on me
    When the rash mood is on.
LEAR No, Regan, thou shalt never have my curse.   45
    Thy tender-hefted nature shall not give
    Thee o'er to harshness. Her eyes are fierce, but thine
    Do comfort and not burn. 'Tis not in thee
    To grudge my pleasures, to cut off my train,
    To bandy hasty words, to scant my sizes,   50
    And in conclusion, to oppose the bolt
    Against my coming in. Thou better know'st
    The offices of nature, bond of childhood,
    Effects of courtesy, dues of gratitude.
    Thy half o'th'kingdom hast thou not forgot   55
    Wherein I thee endowed.
REGAN   Good sir, to th'purpose.
LEAR Who put my man i'th'stocks?

(Act 2 Scene 4, lines 119–75)

Paragraph 1: Locate the extract in the play and identify who is on stage.
Lear has argued with his eldest daughter, Goneril, over the behaviour
of his retinue of knights. As a result he has angrily left her home

intending to seek Regan's hospitality. However, Regan has been forewarned in a letter from her sister and has left home to avoid the need to take Lear in. She and her husband, Cornwall, are already at Gloucester's castle, where this episode takes place. Lear arrives in the castle courtyard and is shocked to find his messenger, Kent, in the stocks. As the extract begins, Kent is still in the stocks, and Lear, his Fool and a Gentleman, are on stage. Lear has sent Gloucester to insist that Regan and Cornwall should come to face him, and awaits their entrance.

Paragraph 2: State what the extract is about and identify its structure.
(Begin with one or two sentences identifying what the extract is about, followed by several sentences briefly identifying its structure, that is, the unfolding events and the different sections of the extract.)

The extract shows the first meeting between Lear and Regan for some time. He hopes to win her sympathy and expects that she will offer lodgings for himself and all his followers. At first Lear complains about the treatment he has received from Goneril, whilst Regan defends her sister. After she orders 'Return you to my sister', Lear curses Goneril and praises Regan. During their conversation, Kent has been released from the stocks: abruptly Lear demands to know who gave the order for that humiliating punishment.

Paragraph 3: Identify the mood or atmosphere of the extract.
The atmosphere of the whole extract is extremely tense. Lear is already in an angry mood, having discovered Kent in the stocks. Quite apart from Kent's personal indignity, this is an insult to Lear himself, and one that has been compounded by Regan's refusal to come to speak with him. When Regan and Cornwall enter, Lear's greeting is sarcastic, but he seems mollified by Cornwall's deferential reply, Regan's more personal response and the immediate release of Kent. Regan's seemingly conciliatory and gentle treatment of her father's concerns in the first section of the extract conceals a dramatic irony. The audience knows that she has read Goneril's version of events in a letter. Although Regan gives a clue to this when she says, 'If, sir, perchance / She have restrained the riots of your followers', Lear does not realise that she has no sympathy for his complaint. Father and daughter become increasingly impatient with one another, until Lear can no longer control his resentment towards Goneril, and shocks

everyone with the vehemence of his curses. Though Lear means to reassure Regan that he thinks well of her, he cannot shake off his mood of indignation, which resurfaces in the question: 'Who put my man i'th'stocks?'

Paragraph 4: Diction (vocabulary)

Many of the words in this extract emphasise the uncompromising natures of the characters. Lear speaks in terms of absolutes: 'Thy sister's naught', 'Never', 'No, Regan, thou shalt never have my curse.' His impulse to control and command is shown through imperatives: 'fall', 'Strike', 'dart', 'Infect'. Regan is outwardly courteous towards her father, prefacing her demands and reprimands with polite phrases such as 'I pray you' and 'Good sir'. However, she shows that she is her father's daughter, using absolutes and imperatives as well as he does: 'clears her from all blame', 'no more', 'Return you' and '[get] to th'purpose'.

There is a double sense in which Regan's sister is 'naught'. In Jacobean times the word meant 'wicked' (from which comes the modern definition of naughty). But in this play 'nothing' has profound significance, and here it is understood that Goneril (like Cordelia) has been reduced to nothing in her father's esteem.

The extract also shows how Shakespeare uses the full range of meanings of a word. 'Nature' is a complex example, which expresses one theme of the play. At lines 20–2, Regan subtly implies that her father is approaching both senility and decrepitude, because everyone is subject to Nature's course of ageing and decay. Lear uses the word 'nature' to mean personality or disposition at line 46, whilst at line 53 he means the loving relationship between child and parent.

Paragraph 5: Imagery

Lear's complaint is that Goneril has disregarded the bond between father and daughter. When he describes the pain this gives him, he uses an animal image: 'she hath tied / Sharp-toothed unkindness, like a vulture here'. The image is one drawn from classical literature, where the Titan Prometheus was punished by the gods for stealing fire from them to give as a gift to the human race. His torture was to be chained to a rock, whilst an eagle devoured his entrails, magically restored each night to be torn from him again the next day. Jacobeans would have recognised the reference to this daily renewable suffering, and perhaps noted too how the eagle, the noble bird of prey of the gods, is here replaced by a hideous carrion-eating vulture.

The use of bestial imagery is a feature of *King Lear*. The simile of the vulture describes the repetitive nature of Lear's torture and emphasises his helplessness against it. The unkindness itself is 'Sharp-toothed', more like a fanged serpent than a hook-beaked vulture, and provides a conceptual link with another simile in the extract. Lear describes how Goneril has verbally abused him: 'struck me with her tongue / Most serpent-like upon the very heart'.

Lear's curses use images of suffering and disease which so frequently recur in the play. He calls down affliction and infection upon his eldest daughter, imagining them being brought by the personified elements: 'taking airs' to make her lame, 'nimble lightnings' to blind her and 'fen-sucked fogs' to disfigure her.

Paragraph 6: Antithesis

Shakespeare uses antithesis to express the conflicts inherent in the episode. When Regan greets her father with apparent gladness, he cannot conceal his conflicting doubts about his standing with his daughter, setting 'I think you are' against 'If thou shouldst not be glad' in lines 3–4. Instead of sympathising at once with her father, Regan defends her sister. When she says, 'You less know how to value her desert / Than she to scant her duty', she sets her sister's motives against Lear's inability to judge what he sees and hears. The syntax of Regan's sentence is tortuous, but the gist is clear and full of irony.

The entire extract expresses antithetical notions. Lear asserts the differences between Regan and her older sister. He sets Goneril's characteristics against Regan's: 'Her eyes are fierce, but thine / Do comfort and not burn.' Describing (and exaggerating) Goneril's actions, he sets word against word ('grudge' against 'pleasures', etc.) to negate that Regan could be so cruel:

> 'Tis not in thee
> To grudge my pleasures, to cut off my train,
> To bandy hasty words, to scant my sizes,
> And in conclusion, to oppose the bolt
> Against my coming in.   *(lines 48–52)*

In contrast he affirms that he believes her to be a more obedient child.

Both the audience and Regan are aware of the stronger similarities between the sisters, and the full irony of Lear's mistaken view will emerge when Regan locks the door against him at the close of this very scene.

Paragraph 7: Repetition

Repetition of words, rhythms and sounds increases the dramatic effect of the extract in different ways. For example, when Lear first addresses Regan, he repeats her name four times. The first of these is in simple greeting, but each new use of the word conveys Lear's growing sense of agitation as he recalls how Goneril has treated him. By the fourth repetition he has become so distraught that he is barely able to gasp out her name 'oh Regan!' Later, Lear calls down the elements in a formal series of invocations: 'Strike . . .', 'dart . . .', 'Infect . . .'. The repeated phrases and patterning give extra force to his commands.

Powerless against his daughter, Lear's hissed anger and defiance is emphasised in the sibilant and stuttering sounds of the words he uses:

> struck me with her tongue
> Most serpent-like upon the very heart.
> All the stored vengeances of heaven fall
> On her ingrateful top! Strike her young bones,
> You taking airs, with lameness.   *(lines 34–8)*

Cornwall's interruption sends Lear into a torrent of alliterative ferocity as the 'f' sound recurs in his cursing: 'flames', 'scornful', 'Infect', 'fen-sucked fogs', 'powerful', 'fall'. Such vitriolic use of language shocks even Regan.

Paragraph 8: Lists

Shakespeare's fondness for piling up items, rather like a list, for different dramatic purposes is also evident in the extract. The list of curses emphasises the excessive nature of Lear's anger. He accumulates Regan's obligations – offices of nature, bond of childhood, effects of courtesy, dues of gratitude – to offer a contrast with the list of unkind actions attributed to Goneril. These two lists approve Regan's character as Lear attempts to win her sympathy, but she remains unpersuaded.

Paragraph 9: Staging opportunities

The focus of the extract is the relationship between Lear and his daughter, Regan. The father appeals to the daughter to ally herself more closely with him: she in turn distances herself from his demands and affections. As the gap in their relationship widens, there is ample opportunity to play out the rift in physical terms. They might come together and even embrace at the start of the extract, yet be separated by the whole width or depth of the stage by the time Regan delivers her icy remark: 'Good sir, to th'purpose.' (Immediately after the extract Regan will turn her back on Lear, to greet her sister warmly.) The way in which Regan acts her part is crucial in this extract where Lear appeals to her better nature, emphasising the differences between her and Goneril. Some productions have made good use of her 'tender-hefted' nature, making her seem kindly towards her father and Gloucester up to this point. Her fake tenderness and insistent concern for Lear might be emphasised here, with the actress adopting a soothing manner, even when what she advises serves her own interests.

The way in which Cornwall and Regan arrive on stage will also make an impact on Lear and on the audience. If they are genuinely weary and clothed in nightgowns, just risen, hurrying, with servants fussing to dress them, the impression can be quite different from a fully-clothed and dignified entrance, with calm attendants.

The extract also addresses an issue which runs through the play: respect for the authority of kings and fathers. Kent's release from the stocks reminds Lear of the insult he has been dealt through this treatment of his servant. The position which Kent takes up on stage will be crucial as a further prompt for Lear to remember how he has been slighted by his daughter and son-in-law. Lear takes the issue a step further when he adopts a deliberately theatrical pose, kneeling before Regan to mock her suggestion that he should return to Goneril. There are several incidents in the play where the king and others kneel; all are significant moments. This is the first time that Lear kneels, and how this is acted may be echoed in later scenes.

Paragraph 10: Conclusion

The extract shows part of the process that drives Lear to his eventual madness. He believes Regan to be dutiful and finds her otherwise, reflecting major themes of the play, deceptive appearances and filial ingratitude. Regan's language is a clear example of the ways in which words can be ambiguous: what she says seems like daughterly good advice, but thinly disguises her exasperation and defiance. Lear struggles to maintain a reasonable response to the emotional blows he receives. The language of his speeches reveals his anxieties and how close he now comes to hysteria. These signs are picked up and used by Regan as proof that he is incapable of governing himself.

Although the division between father and daughter can be strongly emphasised by the staging of this extract, the use of language displays the similarities between Lear and Regan. She is her father's daughter, as imperious, stubborn and self-seeking as he. Her advantage over him at the end of this extract is that she knows the truth about both her own and her sister's intentions for their father. Lear, meanwhile, persists with his incorrect judgements about his children.

Reminders

- The framework is only a guide. It will help you to structure your writing. Use the framework for practice on other extracts. Adapt as you feel appropriate. Make it your own.
- Structure your response in paragraphs. Each paragraph makes a particular point and helps build up your argument.
- Focus tightly on the language, especially vocabulary, imagery, antithesis, lists, repetitions.
- Remember that *King Lear* is a play, a drama intended for performance. The purpose of writing about an extract is to identify how Shakespeare creates dramatic effect. What techniques does he use?
- Try to imagine the action. Visualise the scene in your mind's eye. But remember there can be many valid ways of performing a scene. Offer alternatives. Justify your own preferences by reference to the language.
- Who is on stage? Imagine their interaction. How do 'silent characters' react to what is said?
- Look for the theatrical qualities of the extract. What guides for actors' movement and expressions are given in the language? Comment on any stage directions.

- How might the audience respond? In Jacobean times? Today? How might you respond as a member of the audience?
- How might the lines be spoken? Tone, emphasis, pace, pauses? Identify shifting moods and registers. Is the verse pattern smooth or broken; flowing or full of hesitations and abrupt turns?
- What is the importance of the extract in the play as a whole? Justify its thematic significance.
- Are there any 'key words'?
- How does the extract develop the plot, reveal character, deepen themes?
- In what ways can the extract be spoken/staged to reflect a particular interpretation?

Writing an essay

As part of your study of *King Lear* you will be asked to write essays, either under examination conditions or for coursework (term papers). Examinations mean that you are under pressure of time, usually having around one hour to prepare and write each essay. Coursework means that you have much longer to think about and produce your essay. But whatever the type of essay, each will require you to develop an argument about a particular aspect of *King Lear*.

The essays you write on *King Lear* require that you set out your thoughts on a particular aspect of the play, using evidence from the text. The people who read your essays (examiners, teachers, lecturers) will have certain expectations for your writing. In each essay they will expect you to discuss and analyse a particular topic, using evidence from the play to develop an argument in an organised, coherent and persuasive way. Examiners look for, and reward, what they call 'an informed personal response'. This simply means that you show you have good knowledge of the play ('informed') and can use evidence from it to support and justify your own viewpoint ('personal').

You can write about *King Lear* from different points of view. As pages 91–103 show, you can approach the play from a number of critical perspectives (feminist, political, psychoanalytic, etc.). You can also set the play in its social, literary and other contexts, as shown in the Contexts section. You should write at different levels, moving beyond description to analysis and evaluation. Simply telling the story or describing characters is not as effective as analysing how events or characters embody wider concerns of the play.

In *King Lear*, these 'wider concerns' (also called themes, issues, preoccupations – or more simply 'what the play is about') include appearance versus reality, justice and punishment, relationships between parents and children, blindness and seeing, suffering and disease, nature, madness. In your writing, always give practical examples (quotations, actions) which illustrate the themes you discuss.

How should you answer an examination question or write a coursework essay? The following three-fold structure can help you organise your response:

opening paragraph
developing paragraphs
concluding paragraph

Opening paragraph. Begin with a paragraph identifying what topic or issue you will focus on. Show that you have understood what the question is about. You probably will have prepared for particular topics. But look closely at the question and identify key words to see what particular aspect it asks you to write about. Adapt your material to answer that question. Examiners do not reward an essay, however well written, if it is not on the question set.

Developing paragraphs. This is the main body of your essay. In it, you develop your argument, point by point, paragraph by paragraph. Use evidence from the play that illuminates the topic or issue, and answers the question set. Each paragraph makes a point of dramatic or thematic significance. Some paragraphs could make points concerned with context or particular critical approaches. The effect of your argument builds up as each paragraph adds to the persuasive quality of your essay. Use brief quotations that support your argument, and show clearly just why they are relevant. Ensure that your essay demonstrates that you are aware that *King Lear* is a play; a drama intended for performance, and therefore open to a wide variety of interpretations and audience response.

> *Concluding paragraph.* Your final paragraph pulls together your main conclusions. It does not simply repeat what you have written earlier, but summarises concisely how your essay has successfully answered the question.

Example

> Question: 'All's cheerless, dark, and deadly.' How far do you agree with Kent's assessment of the end of the play?

The following notes show the 'ingredients' of an answer, given here in note form. In an examination it is usually helpful to prepare similar notes from which you write your essay, paragraph by paragraph. To help you understand how contextual matters or points from different critical approaches might be included, the words 'Context' or 'Criticism' appear before some items. Remember that Examiners are not impressed by 'name-dropping': use of critics' names without showing relevance to your point. What they want you to show is your knowledge and judgement of the play and its contexts, and of how it has been interpreted from different critical perspectives.

Opening paragraph
Show that you know what the question is asking by identifying the moment when Kent speaks these words. Put them into context, perhaps even rephrase them for clarity. Notice that the question asks you to give your opinion on whether the quotation provides a reasonable description of the ending of the play. So you must decide: is the play 'cheerless, dark, and deadly' or not? State your view and give brief initial reasons. You might include any of the following points, with one or more sentences on each:

- The quotation identifies a particular view of the play (nihilistic).
- It implies there is no redemption, no hope, that the remaining characters can have no impact on the future.
- It seems to justify the fatalistic view of Gloucester regarding Fortune, fate, doom.

- Criticism: There are, however, other ways of looking at the play (redemptive, Christian, etc.).
- Criticism: performance The stage is littered with dead bodies.

Developing paragraphs

Write one paragraph on each of a number of different ways in which the play might be interpreted. In each paragraph identify the importance (dramatic, thematic, etc.) of any examples or quotations you discuss. Some of the points you might include are given briefly below.

- The problem of Cordelia – given that she is so 'good', how can her death be just? (See what Dr Johnson had to say about the ending, page 84.)
- The puzzle of Edgar – is he a suitable candidate to rule the kingdom? (Perhaps compare with other plays' endings, e.g. Young Fortinbras in *Hamlet*.)
- Context: Is there any sense in which Shakespeare presents a traditionally tragic ending? Is Lear's character 'flawed'? Does the play offer catharsis (in which pity and fear purge the emotions)?
- Context: How might the Jacobeans have viewed the ending in terms of the politics of the day? (The notion of dividing a kingdom was abhorrent to King James.)
- Criticism: There are differences in interpretation: for some critics, the play is dark and nihilistic (e.g. the despairing comment of Gloucester: 'As flies to wanton boys are we to th'gods'; an apocalyptic ending – 'Is this the promised end? Or image of that horror?'). Others see the play as a Christian story of redemption (e.g. seeing Cordelia as Christ-like, Lear as redeemed through humiliation and suffering).
- Criticism: performance Rarely performed in the seventeenth century, until Nahum Tate's happy ending version reflecting tastes of the time. (Restoration of original demonstrates changed attitudes towards the play and its preoccupations, finding modern relevances in its horrors.)
- Criticism: performance How have recent performances interpreted the ending? (Mention some that you know of from stage or screen, describing how they present the final moments of the play.)

Concluding paragraph

Write several sentences pulling together your conclusions. Whether the ending is 'cheerless, dark, and deadly' might depend on what Kent sees on stage and on what Lear sees (or refuses to see), so be sure that you have discussed that. You may want also to give your view on political issues or the nihilist/redemptivist counter-arguments. Perhaps you will feel the need to comment on the director or producer's licence to enforce a certain interpretation.

Whatever else your conclusion contains you must describe the extent to which you agree with the question, now that you have explored the issue. What have your arguments led you to?

- You might agree with Kent wholly – give a final convincing reason.
- You might disagree entirely – give your main reason.
- You might consider the issue too complex to be resolved definitely – give a few brief reasons why.

Writing about character

As the Critical approaches section showed, much critical writing about *King Lear* traditionally focused on characters, writing about them as if they were living human beings. Today it is not sufficient just to describe their personalities. When you write about characters, you will also be expected to show that they are dramatic constructs, part of Shakespeare's stagecraft. They embody the wider concerns of the play, have certain dramatic functions, and are set in a social and political world with particular values and beliefs. They reflect and express issues of significance to Shakespeare's society – and today's.

All that may seem difficult and abstract. But don't feel overwhelmed. Everything you read in this Guide is written with those principles in mind, and can be a model for your own writing. Of course you should say what a character seems like to you, but you should also write about how Shakespeare makes him or her part of his overall dramatic design. For example:

- Kent and Edgar have similar dramatic functions. Each is in some way banished, each takes on a disguise in order to protect others. Both display enduring loyalty and can be seen as the moral lynchpins of the play.
- Lear and Gloucester have marked similarities. Both fathers fail to

'see' their children clearly, both suffer terribly for their errors. Finally each achieves insight and self-knowledge and is reconciled with his 'good' child. Gloucester's blinding is a visual reminder of both characters' lack of perception.

- Edgar and Edmund contrast with one another. Edmund's evil nature is strongly charismatic, in sharp and ironic contrast to the bland goodness of his brother Edgar.
- Albany and Cornwall are also contrasting characters, emphasising the dichotomy between good and evil. When Lear divides his kingdom there seems little to choose between them. But as the play progresses they become divided in loyalties and actions, emphasising the difference in their moral status.
- The Fool provides sardonic commentary on the words and actions of Lear and other characters. His jests and songs reveal the consequences of Lear's folly and the nature of his daughters.

Another way of thinking of characters is that in Shakespeare's time, playwrights and audiences were less concerned with psychological realism than with character types and their functions. That is, they expected and recognised such stock figures of traditional drama as the scheming Machiavellian or dissatisfied malcontent (Edmund), the faithful counsellor (Gloucester and Kent), the tragic hero who must suffer (Lear), and the personified vices and virtues of morality plays, such as Vanity (Goneril), Lust (Regan and Goneril), Truth (Cordelia) and Vice itself (Edmund).

But there is a danger in writing about the functions of characters or the character types they represent. To reduce a character to a mere plot device is just as inappropriate as treating him or her as a real person. When you write about characters in *King Lear* you should try to achieve a balance between analysing their personality, identifying the dilemmas they face, showing how they change or develop in the course of the play, and placing them in their social, critical and dramatic contexts. That style of writing is found all through this Guide, and that, together with the following brief discussions, can help your own written responses to character.

Lear. Although Lear emerges as a tragic figure, he does not easily fit the simple description of the tragic hero. It is not a single 'tragic flaw' or error of judgement that causes his downfall, even though he does undergo a journey from ignorance to self-knowledge characteristic of many tragic heroes. Regan's remark that 'he hath ever but slenderly known himself' seems a perceptive assessment of her father in the early stages of the play. Soon afterwards, rejected by his eldest daughter, he begins to search for that knowledge, asking 'Who is it that can tell me who I am?' The Fool's answer 'Lear's shadow', has led some critics to doubt whether Lear ever becomes more than the shadow of his former kingly self.

Lear's encounter with the blinded Gloucester, and his reconciliation with Cordelia, show that he has learned through his suffering. Yet his self-knowledge is still partial, and even with his madness gone, he lacks full understanding that he has been the agent of his own misfortunes, unable to shake free of the role he earlier cast for himself, 'a man / More sinned against than sinning', a victim of circumstance. The key to Lear's character lies in his language (see pages 75–6). Although the 'love trial' of the first scene shows him to be infuriatingly blind to reality, uncompromising in his will and unjust in his decisions, he is loved, by Cordelia, by Kent and by the Fool. In the final scene of the play Lear dies as a father, not as a tyrant, his focus no longer inward and self-seeking but outward, towards Cordelia, 'Look there, look there.' Whether he dies in hope that she lives is open to every reader and audience member to decide.

Goneril. Lear's eldest daughter in her very first speech, polished and evidently rehearsed, is unable to hide completely her deviousness. Her later complaint to her father over his retinue seems superficially reasonable, but it too masks a corrupt intention. She rejects her father, plots adultery and worse against her husband and poisons her sister in the pursuit of political power and sexual gratification. Some critics have been reminded of Lady Macbeth as Goneril lays plans, adopts a dominant role and mocks her husband. He reviles her, calling her a devil but Goneril simply brushes off his remarks. At the end of the play, her plans thwarted and faced with an ignominious end, she stabs herself.

Regan. Initially, Lear's second daughter might seem a more sympathetic character than her elder sister. But she quickly reveals that her true disposition is more cruel than her sister's. Vicious, she delights in torturing those who oppose her will. She extends Kent's punishment in the stocks, unfeelingly denies her father any followers ('What need one?'), orders that the doors of Gloucester's castle should be shut against Lear, and when Cornwall puts out one of Gloucester's eyes, she pitilessly urges that 'One side will mock another: th'other, too.' Regan is as ambitious, adulterous and greedy as her older sister, and at times unnervingly like her father, in the imperious style of her language, as when she defends Edmund's claims. For a woman with such a treacherous and poisonous nature, poison might seem a fitting death. The two sisters, so often described in bestial terms – 'dog-hearted', 'pelican daughters', with 'wolvish fangs' – meet with brutal ends.

Cordelia. Although a major character and the catalyst for much of the action, Cordelia speaks in only four scenes. Her femininity and gentleness are emphasised, in contrast to the personalities of her sisters, but she is not weak. She speaks the truth to her father in the face of his anger, and she later leads an invading army. The traditional view of Cordelia has been that she is 'blameless', without responsibility for the tragedy that befalls her father, but that view has often been challenged. Whilst some critics have found her piety annoying, others have admired her integrity. Cordelia despises hypocrisy and pretence: commenting on Regan's excessive flattery she says, 'I am sure my love's / More ponderous than my tongue'. However, her conviction that she is right makes her uncompromising, and she refuses to humour her father. She and the Fool are Lear's two most precious creatures. Lear himself makes the link between them when, with Cordelia's lifeless body in his arms, he says 'my poor fool is hanged'. Some productions have enhanced this relationship further still by 'doubling' the characters. In a play that so sharply portrays the clear polarities of good and evil characters, Cordelia is the supreme representative of the good. In her resides the audience's hope that justice will prevail and right will triumph. In her death, Shakespeare shatters that hope: it is small wonder that Nahum Tate's alternative version of *King Lear*, in which Cordelia lives on, remained popular with audiences for over 150 years.

The Fool. Fools were often employed in the palaces of royalty or great houses of noble families. Although they had the title of 'fool' (or jester or clown), they were much more intelligent than foolish ('a wise fool'). Their job was not to provide humour in the physical, boisterous way of clowns, but to amuse courtiers with their critical comment on contemporary behaviour. An 'allowed' or 'licensed' fool was permitted to say what he thought, a privilege often denied even to a ruler's closest counsellors. Lear's Fool, however, is not as simple as this stock characterisation suggests. True, he delivers much of his fool's wisdom in a choric style, commentating on the action around him, advising Lear and others and dispensing 'wise' sayings which are not 'throwaways' or mere jingles but provide insight into certain of the play's crucial issues. The difference between Lear's Fool and the stock character is that he can appear as either 'sweet' or 'bitter' – or both! The Fool has been seen as Lear's guardian angel, the voice of common sense, and even Lear's conscience. His relationship with his master is a close and poignant one. Yet the Fool disappears from the play, departing with 'And I'll go to bed at noon' at the end of Act 3 Scene 6. Whether the Fool has done all he can for Lear, or considers himself outfooled by the counterfeiters and madmen around him, the question of why Shakespeare dispensed with him is not fully resolved.

Kent. Kent is a constant presence in two ways. First, he appears on stage for approximately half of the play, more than any other character, casting a watchful eye over his master or doing his bidding. Secondly he is constant in his loyalty towards Lear. Kent's qualities are his faithfulness and his plain speaking, but they also lead him into difficulties. Unlike his master, he recognises cunning and flattery when he sees and hears it. He is not afraid to defend truth and plain speaking: 'To plainness honour's bound, / When majesty falls to folly.' (Act 1 Scene 1, lines 142–3).

He is a plain speaker by craft and not by accident, as when he demonstrates to Cornwall that he can use the language of flattery, but that he chooses not to. He is, therefore, an unusual courtier in that when he practises deception through disguise, it is not for his own gain, but for the good of others, as he works to restore Lear and Cordelia to their rightful places.

Gloucester. Lear's other long-standing counsellor reveals himself as a sensualist as he jokes about how Edmund was conceived. He falls into the same trap as the king, quite mistaking the true moral natures of his children. Gloucester fails to look for the truth about Edgar and blindly casts him off. In ironic return for this sin he suffers physical blinding before he comes to realise: 'I stumbled when I saw'. Unlike Lear, he finds it hard to endure his punishment, and attempts suicide at Dover, then sinks into despair. Edgar tries to make him realise that he must acquire patience before his spiritual wounds will heal, but Gloucester finds it hard to learn.

Edgar is a righteous deceiver. His disguises and tricks, whilst preserving his own life, help both Lear and Gloucester towards self-knowledge. They also bring Edmund to justice. At the end of the play, Edgar is offered rule of the kingdom, which he accepts. His qualification for kingship, apart from the fact that he is Lear's godson, seems to be that of the surviving characters he alone has the will and energy to rule.

In contrast, **Edmund** has much more audience appeal, partly established by his speaking directly to the audience in soliloquies and asides. He is dynamic with a strong physical presence. His leadership qualities are appreciated by Cornwall, and his sexual attractiveness by Regan and Goneril. His dark nature (like that of later anti-heroes, such as Milton's Satan, or Darth Vader) does not make him likeable, but is compelling. He is an arch-deceiver, a Machiavellian. Rather than targeting a few victims, he beguiles everyone. He is completely self-seeking and unashamedly so, as his asides and soliloquies reveal. No spark of kindness resides in him, but in an uncharacteristic moment in the final scene, at the point of death, he says 'Some good I mean to do, / Despite of mine own nature.' Critics disagree on whether Edmund has been 'humanised' by hearing the story of his father's death and sufferings. There seems strong support for the view that he remains evil. When his death is announced it is considered 'a trifle'.

Cornwall and Albany. Cornwall, husband to Regan, is described as 'fiery', the 'hot duke' whose impetuous anger can lead to the utmost cruelty. He shows brazen disrespect towards his father-in-law when he puts his messenger into the stocks, and his sadistic treatment of Gloucester is vile. He has all the makings of a tyrant, and the news of his death is greeted by Albany (and audiences) with relief:

> This shows you are above,
> You justicers, that these our nether crimes
> So speedily can venge.   *(Act 4 Scene 2, lines 47–9)*

Albany seems dominated by his wife, Goneril, in the earlier scenes, but develops more powerfully as the play progresses. He is reported to regret his involvement with the evil characters against Lear. After an absence of thirteen scenes, his change of heart is almost complete and he directly confronts Goneril with her misdemeanours. Yet Albany is a procrastinator. Though he subscribes to the cause of right and truth, he still cannot make a clean break from his old allies until the battle has been fought. At the end of the play Albany, as the highest ranking survivor, should assume the role of ruler, and by dramatic tradition speak the final lines of the play. Characteristically, he relinquishes the responsibility for both to Edgar.

A note on examiners

Examiners do not try to trap you or trick you. They set questions and select passages for comment intended to help you write your own informed personal response to the play. They expect your answer to display a sound knowledge and understanding of the play, and to be well structured. They want you to develop an argument, using evidence from the text to support your interpretations and judgements. Examiners know there is never one 'right answer' to a question, but always opportunities to explore different approaches and interpretations. They welcome answers which directly address the question set, and which demonstrate originality, insight and awareness of complexity. Above all, they reward responses which show your awareness that *King Lear* is a play for performance, and that you can identify how Shakespeare achieves his dramatic effects.

And what about critics? Examiners want you to show you are aware of different critical approaches to the play. But they do not expect you simply to drop critics' names into your essay, or to remember quotations from critics. Rather, they want you to show that you can interpret the play from different critical perspectives, and that you know that any critical approach provides only a partial view of *King Lear*. Often, that need only be just a section of your essay. In your writing, examiners are always interested centrally in your view of the play, and in how you have come to that view from thinking critically about the play, reading it, reading about it, seeing it performed, and perhaps from acting some of it yourself – even if that acting takes place in your imagination!

Resources

Books

A C Bradley, *Shakespearean Tragedy*, Penguin 1991
Originally published in 1904, this is the most important source of 'character criticism'. Even though Bradley's approach is much criticised, his clear style and close reading, and identification of crucial questions about *King Lear* can yield valuable insights.

H B Charlton, *Shakespearean Tragedy*, Methuen 1948
A clearly written introduction, mainly concerned with character, but calling for a synthesis of approaches to the tragedies.

John F Danby, *Shakespeare's Doctrine of Nature: A study of King Lear*, Faber 1969
A searching exploration of the play through two different views of nature: benign and malignant.

Jonathan Dollimore, *Radical Tragedy: Religion, Ideology and Power in the Drama of Shakespeare and His Contemporaries*, 2nd edition, Harvester Wheatsheaf 1989
The book makes heavy demands on readers, but argues persuasively that *King Lear* and other Jacobean tragedies are critical of the society of their time.

Terry Eagleton, *William Shakespeare*, Basil Blackwell 1986
Although Eagleton includes only a few pages on *King Lear*, his book exemplifies postmodern (or deconstructive) approaches to Shakespeare's plays.

W R Elton, *King Lear and the Gods*, Huntingdon Library, San Marino 1966
Argues strongly against interpretations of *King Lear* as a Christian-like drama of redemption through suffering, seeing it as one which 'shatters . . . the foundations of faith itself'.

Barbara Everett, 'The new King Lear', in Frank Kermode (ed.), *Shakespeare, King Lear: A Casebook*, Macmillan 1969
An influential essay that expresses scepticism about readings of *King Lear* as a Christian morality play.

Howard Felperin, 'Plays within Plays', in Kiernan Ryan (ed.), *King Lear: New Casebooks*, Macmillan 1993
An extract from *Shakespearean Representation: Mimesis and Modernity in Elizabethan Tragedy*, Princeton 1977, one of the first postmodern readings of Shakespeare. Argues that in *King Lear* Shakespeare 'leaves us in the end with not a choice of *either* morality or meaning *or* madness and absurdity, but more like an ultimatum of *neither* morality and meaning *nor* madness and absurdity'.

Jonathan Goldberg, 'Dover Cliff and the conditions of Representation', in Kiernan Ryan (ed.), *King Lear: New Casebooks*, Macmillan 1993
A postmodern reading that sees Edgar's imagined Dover as 'a working out of illusion that rests on nothing: silence, invisibility, blindness'.

Harley Granville Barker, *Prefaces to Shakespeare*, Batsford 1972
A highly influential reading by a theatre practitioner. Essential for students of stagecraft. Granville Barker, himself a playwright and director, gives prescriptive advice on staging and characterisation, and firmly rejects the claims of Lamb and Bradley that *King Lear* cannot be effectively presented on stage.

Coppelia Kahn, 'The absent mother in *King Lear*', in Kiernan Ryan (ed.), *King Lear: New Casebooks*, Macmillan 1993
A psychoanalytic and historical perspective on the play which argues for 'Lear's progress toward acceptance of the woman in himself'.

Frank Kermode (ed.), *Shakespeare, King Lear: A Casebook*, Macmillan 1969
A very helpful collection of criticism of the play, including extracts from Bradley, Wilson Knight, Elton, Kott, Welsford, and Everett noted in this booklist.

Frank Kermode, *Shakespeare's Language*, Allen Lane, Penguin 2000
A detailed examination of how Shakespeare's language changed over the course of his playwriting career. Contains an excellent chapter on *King Lear*, and the discussion of other plays can also illuminate understanding of Shakespeare's use of language.

Victor Kiernan, *Eight Tragedies of Shakespeare: A Marxist Study*, Verso 1996
Contains a radical, social reading of *King Lear* which sees only 'forlorn hope' at the end of the play, but which argues that 'a few individuals can defy the force of social gravity', and that humanity can survive and move forward.

G Wilson Knight, *The Wheel of Fire*, Methuen 1949 (first published 1930)
Two chapters on *King Lear*, '*King Lear* and the Comedy of the Grotesque', and 'The Lear Universe' argue that Christian values and doctrines are evident in the play.

Jan Kott, *Shakespeare our Contemporary*, Methuen 1965
An influential political reading of Shakespeare's plays. The chapter '*King Lear*, or *Endgame*' sees *Lear* as similar to the absurdity of the plays of Samuel Beckett.

Kathleen McLuskie, 'The Patriarchal Bard: Feminist criticism and *King Lear*', in Kiernan Ryan (ed.), *King Lear: New Casebooks*, Macmillan 1993
Assuming that tragedy is a reactionary genre, McLuskie's polemical essay claims that *King Lear* is a misogynistic representation of women.

Michael Mangan, *A Preface to Shakespeare's Tragedies*, Longman 1991
Provides helpful material on historical and political contexts.

Kenneth Muir (ed.), *Shakespeare Survey 33*, Cambridge University Press 1980
The essays by Derek Peat (on the play's ending), and G R Hibbard (on critical approaches 1939–79) are particularly helpful.

James Ogden and **Arthur H Scouten** (eds.), *Lear from Study to Stage*, Associated University Presses 1997
A very readable collection which includes essays on recent criticism (Richard Levin), *Lear* on film (Anthony Davies) and female characters (Carol Rutter).

Kiernan Ryan (ed.), *King Lear: New Casebooks*, Macmillan 1993
A valuable collection of modern criticism: political, feminist, psychiatric and post-structuralist. Contains extracts from or essays by Eagleton, Felperin, Goldberg, Kahn, McLuskie and Ryan mentioned in this booklist.

Kiernan Ryan, '*King Lear*: the subversive imagination', in Kiernan Ryan (ed.), *King Lear: New Casebooks*, Macmillan 1993
A radical humanist reading that argues *King Lear* subverts the status quo and provides 'a repressed hunger for liberating transformation'.

Caroline Spurgeon, *Shakespeare's Imagery and What it Tells Us*, Cambridge University Press 1935
The first major study of imagery in the plays. Although much criticised today, Spurgeon's identification of image clusters as a dominant feature of the plays has influenced later studies.

Gary Taylor and **Michael Warren** (eds.), *The Division of the Kingdoms: Shakespeare's Two Versions of King Lear*, Clarendon Press 1983
See especially the chapters by Stanley Wells ('The Once and Future King Lear'), John Kerrigan ('Revision, adaptation and the Fool in *King Lear*'), and Thomas Clayton (' "Is this the promised end?": Revision in the Role of the King').

Enid Welsford, 'The Fool in *King Lear*', in Frank Kermode (ed.), *Shakespeare, King Lear: A Casebook*, Macmillan 1969
Sets Lear's Fool in the historical and social context of medieval and Tudor England.

Films

Film versions usually available on video include:

1971 *King Lear* Director: Peter Brook. Lear: Paul Scofield.
A Royal Shakespeare Company production in which the bleakness of interpretation is reflected in the harsh landscape. Brook seizes every opportunity to bring out the savagery of the play. For example, Cordelia's hanging is shown, and Goneril kills Regan by banging her head against a rock, then kills herself in the same way. Critical reactions have ranged from 'a masterpiece' to 'a travesty'. Perhaps the most representative judgement is that Brook's film possesses 'a kind of fractured greatness'.

1971 *King Lear* Director: Grigori Kozintsev. Lear: Yuri Yarvet.
A Russian film in which the common people are a striking presence. The film opens with hundreds of peasants outside Lear's castle. When he appears, they kneel to him as if he were a god. The hovel on the heath is crowded with poor people, and the battle in which Cordelia and Lear are defeated results in a tide of frightened refugees.

1982 *King Lear* Director: Jonathan Miller. Lear: Michael Horden.
Made for the BBC television Shakespeare series.

1983 *King Lear* Director: Michael Elliot. Lear: Laurence Olivier.
A television production set in ninth-century Britain.

1985 *Ran* Director: Akira Kurosawa. Lear (named Hidetora Ichimondi): Tatsuya Nakadai.
A highly acclaimed Japanese adaptation, set in sixteenth-century Japan, full of dazzling images and thrilling spectacle. Instead of three daughters, there are three sons. In Japanese, *Ran* means 'chaos' or 'desolation of the soul'.

The characters and plot of *King Lear* have provided the inspiration for a number of screen adaptations. These include:

1954 *Broken Lance* A cowboy film in which the youngest son of a cattleman fights his brothers who have divided up their dead father's ranch.

1983 *The Dresser* This film of Ronald Harwood's play of the same title seems based on the relationship between King Lear and his Fool. The central characters are an aged actor and his dresser. The actor tours English provincial theatres as Lear. His dresser has the same mordant wit as the Fool. At the end of the film the actor dies just after his onstage death as Lear.

1997 *A Thousand Acres* This adaptation of Jane Smiley's novel is set in modern Iowa. A prosperous farmer divides his thousand acres between his three daughters, but rejects the youngest when she challenges his decision.

Audio books
Four major versions are available, in the series by Naxos, Arkangel, HarperCollins and BBC Radio Collection.

King Lear on the Web
If you type 'King Lear Shakespeare' into your search engine, it may find more than 100,000 items. Because websites are of wildly varying quality, and rapidly disappear or are created, no recommendation can safely be made. But if you have time to browse, you may find much of interest.